Dedication

To my husband, Mark, my children and their spouses, Stacey, David, Brooke, and Jason, and my grandchildren, Julia and James, for being a constant source of encouragement and support. You never let me give up and were with me every step of the way. God has truly blessed me through you.

To the women of the Wetzel Road church of Christ Wednesday evening Bible study, for your steadfast encouragement and willingness to be my "guinea pigs" with the material. Your feedback was invaluable.

To Doris Coomey, I wish you were here to see what you started when you first gave me that push years ago.

Most of all, to God, without whom these words and thoughts would not have found their way into print for others to read and experience. To God be all the glory.

BOLD Devotion

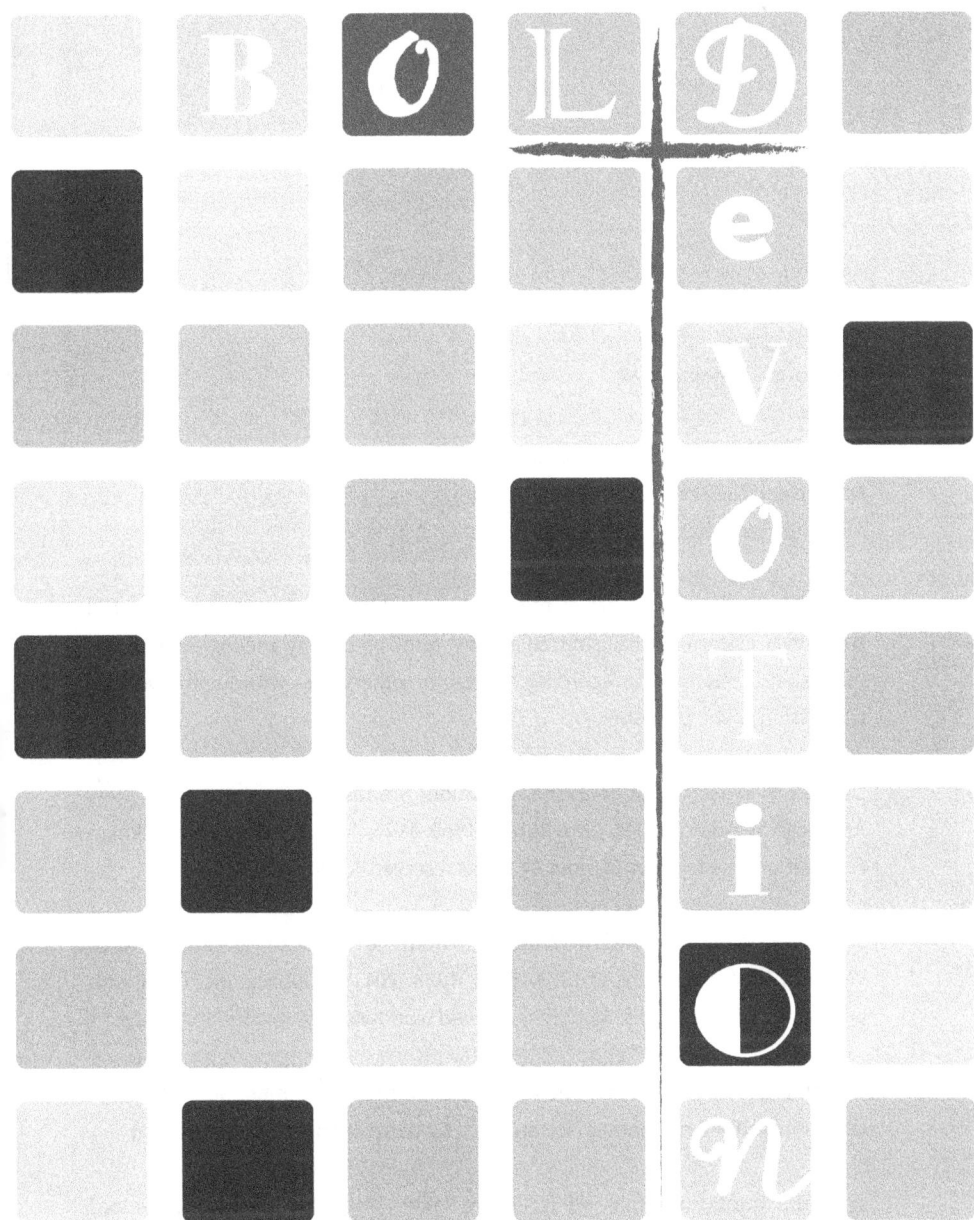

LINDA CONDOLORA

21ST CENTURY CHRISTIAN

Table of Contents

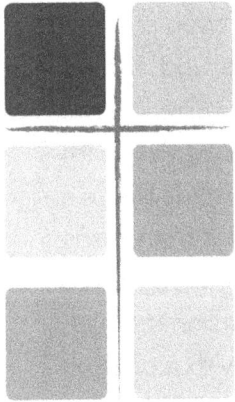

1

Bear His Image

Who do you look like? From the day you were born, you've resembled one of your parents. It might be your eyes or nose, your mannerisms or facial expressions, or all of the above, but you always look like one or both of them. You don't have a choice in the matter. Your genes decide for you.

When you became a Christian, you experienced another birth — a rebirth (1 Peter 1:3). Think back to when you came up out of the waters of baptism, a new creation in Christ Jesus. You looked the same, but everything was different. Maybe you felt excitement, relief, peace, or joy. Whatever your feelings, you looked forward to your new life in Christ. You were changed, and this new life was exciting. The major difference between your physical birth and your spiritual birth was, and is, that you now get to decide who you look like.

In the days immediately following my spiritual birth, I remember living life intentionally — focused on being like Christ. I was aware of the words I used, how I treated others, and that I had an intense desire to share the good news about Jesus. Do you remember the zeal you had and the effort you put into being like Jesus? Our shared goal was to please God and be obedient to Him. Somewhere along the way, if you're like me, you lost the eagerness and zeal you had for sharing Him with others. It wasn't a conscious decision either of us made to live a lukewarm Christian life, looking more like ourselves than Jesus, but it happened nonetheless. It's time for us, once again, to decide who we want to look like — the lukewarm version to which we've become accustomed or the person filled with a passion for God, desiring to reflect Jesus to the world? I know which one I'm choosing, and I hope you'll join me as we rediscover how to live and look like Jesus.

Looking Like Jesus

Saying I want to live and look like Jesus is easy; living a Christian life filled with a passion for God and His purposes is not. What does being passionate about something look like? Let me share an example that has nothing to do with God but is an excellent illustration. A few years ago, I was in the kitchen, frying meatballs, when my adult daughter and mother of two stopped in. She was excited because the 90s pop band, Hanson, was coming to town on New Year's Eve. As I listened, I saw once again the 15-year-old who'd incessantly played Hanson's hit single, "MMMBop," on her stereo. All those years ago, she had begged me to let her go to their concert in Albany, New York, with her aunt and cousin. The passion with which she had pleaded for my permission then reminded me so much of how she was speaking now, that it brought a smile to my face.

When New Year's Eve arrived, it was only 10 degrees outside with a minus 10-degree windchill. I thought she might change her mind about going to this outdoor concert, but she and my daughter-in-law left the house with their excitement to keep them warm. They stood in the freezing cold, with many other folks, for three hours, just to hear their childhood heartthrobs perform. Not even their frozen faces and slightly frostbitten toes could dampen their spirits. That's passion. And it's the passion I want to have for Jesus and the Christian life again — a passion that makes me willing to sacrifice and be uncomfortable for the God in whom I have placed my faith.

Looking around us, we see people who are passionate about many things — exercise, music, politics, and sports. But there is one thing that everyone cares about, and that is image — how they look to others. Since they say confession is good for the soul, I'll confess that I, too, have fallen for this.

One day, when I was in the middle of making dinner (okay, it was cookies), I discovered I was out of one ingredient. I immediately got in my car and drove to the grocery store. Because I was in a hurry, I left my house without thinking of my appearance. To be honest, I don't even think I had brushed my hair that day. I'm not exaggerating when I tell you I was quite the sight. As I turned down a store aisle, I noticed a woman ahead whom I knew, and my thoughts immediately went to how I looked. Making a fast U-turn, I quickly left the aisle, hoping she hadn't seen me. How I looked certainly mattered to me at that moment!

Though this example is silly, it illustrates something serious. In our culture, concern with image is a serious issue that has birthed an entire industry called image consulting. Something being true or not no longer matters. The most important thing is how it looks, because image sells. We don't mean to, but we fall into the same image trap as the world. All women, including Christians, face a barrage of pictures and messages in magazines, on television, radio, and the internet of how we should look, act, and think. Sadly, many of these messages and attitudes are contrary to what the Bible teaches, and too often, we fall prey to them.

Getting caught up in wearing the latest fashions and hairstyles like the rest of the world means we spend loads of time and money making ourselves appealing and acceptable. We worry about what others think of us when they see us. Why else did I turn down a grocery aisle to avoid running into someone I knew? Worse than that, we often make snap judgments about others based on the way they look.

The world's messages and attitudes affect us, but not just in physical appearance. If we let it, our concern about appearance dampens our passion to look and be like Jesus. Our desire to fit in often leads us to keep our thoughts to ourselves. Have you ever been talking with co-workers when they discuss a societal issue that God has clearly said is sinful? The rest of the group is saying that it's okay and people who disagree are just intolerant or ignorant. Do you say anything? If not, why not?

Fear of rejection and being left out are powerful deterrents to sharing our faith. My granddaughter, at eight-years-old, was talking about giving her life to Jesus. She said to me, "Grandma, I know that if I become a Christian, I might have to die for Jesus. And I know I might be persecuted for my belief in Jesus. I might lose some of my friends because of my belief. But that's okay. I just love Jesus and want to live for Him. I love Jesus so much." Wow! That's the attitude I had as a new Christian, and it's the attitude I long to live by for the rest of my life.

Losing that passion and determination to reflect Jesus through our lives happens so gradually that we don't even notice. My theory is that our spiritual lenses slowly become aimed in the wrong direction. Though they used to be aimed squarely at

God's Word and what He accepts and expects, little by little, we unwittingly widen our lenses to include the world's values. When we do that, the lines blur, and eventually, the picture grows fuzzy. The only way to refocus the image of God, Jesus, and Christianity is to point our lenses back in God's direction. If we want to know what God thinks about anything, the Bible is the place to go. It's time to refocus our lenses on God's Word.

Looking Back

When writing this chapter, listening for God's leading, I opened the Bible and started reading where my eyes landed on the page. "As these men were going away, Jesus began to speak to the crowds about John, 'What did you go out into the wilderness to see?'" (Matthew 11:7, NASB 95)

I continued reading. "What did you go out into the wilderness to see? A reed shaken by the wind? But what did you go out to see? A man dressed in soft clothing? Those who wear soft clothing are in kings' palaces! But what did you go out to see? A prophet? Yes, I tell you, and one who is more than a prophet. This is the one about whom it is written, 'Behold, I send my messenger ahead of you, who will prepare your way before you'" (Matthew 11:7-10).

Jesus asked three times, "What did you go out into the desert to see?" Does that make you wonder what they *did* go out to see? It made me wonder, so I took a trip to the desert, through the pages of Scripture, to witness what they saw when they came upon John. Take a few minutes now to take your own trek to the desert by reading Matthew 3:1-15. Go ahead. I'll wait for you.

Were you able to look through 2,000-year-old eyes and see the man they called John the Baptist? Did you see a man in fine clothes? Well, unless you consider rough, smelly, camel hair to be fine clothes, then no. How about a man of wealth and refinement? Not unless you enjoy feasting on locusts and honey. So, what made people travel long distances to see John? Bear with me, as I quote from Matthew 3:7-10: "But when he saw many of the Pharisees and Sadducees coming for baptism, he said to them, 'You brood of vipers, who warned you to flee from the wrath to come? Therefore bear fruit in keeping with repentance; and do not suppose that you can say to yourselves, "We have Abraham for our father"; for I say to you that from these stones God is able to raise up children to Abraham. The axe is already laid at the root of the trees; therefore every tree that does not bear good fruit is cut down and thrown into the fire.'"

There's the answer. People went to the desert to see and hear a man of passion. Put on those 2,000-year-old glasses again, and look closer at John. He is a man living in the desert on locusts and honey and wearing camel hides for clothing. If looks were all that mattered, you would probably turn away. But oh, when he speaks, you can't help being drawn to him. As you listen, he transforms before your eyes. You no longer see the disheveled man or wrinkle your nose at his stench. This man, John, has something important to say, and he isn't afraid to say it, even to the Jewish religious leaders. Listen. Hear the passion in his words. See him pointing his finger at them, shouting, "You brood of vipers!" Jesus is right. John is no reed shaken by the wind. He is a man of God, a prophet. He has a message directly from God, and he will be heard. As we look at John with our 21st-century eyes, we see he was nothing like the politicians of today. John didn't need any polls. He knew who he was, to whom he belonged, and what he believed. John wouldn't water down his message or change for anyone. He was a devoted servant of God.

Yes, John was a passionate man, but if we look again at Matthew 3:13-15, we discover he was more than that. In these verses, if we look beyond his appearance, we see another John — the faithful and humble John. He is shocked that

Jesus has come to him to be baptized and responds, "I have need to be baptized by you." Some might have felt proud being chosen by Jesus to baptize Him, but not John. He knew his place before Christ and gave Him the respect and obedience He deserved. The people went out to the desert to see the strange man, dressed in equally strange clothing, but once there, they saw a completely different image — one that touched their hearts and changed their lives — a man of passion mixed with humility. John never looked for the adoration or honor of men; he didn't want them looking at him. He never lost sight of his purpose, to point people to Jesus, which he did with passionate words and a fervent faith.

You may think, *What does John fulfilling his purpose have to do with me and my image?* It is important for us to study John because we also are to point people to Jesus. Remember the passion and excitement you had at first. Your passion poured out naturally as you shared Christ with others. But over time, the passion dissipates, life interrupts, and our own image obscures the image of Jesus. When we become more concerned about how we look to people rather than whether they see Jesus in us, our lives become out of focus.

I became a Christian during a summer break from college. Full of excitement and newfound understanding, I wanted everyone to know Jesus. When I returned to college in the fall, my passion and zeal led me to share what I'd learned with all of my friends. Unfortunately, though I had the passion of John, I was missing the humility to balance it. Instead of the message of Christ's love, what my friends heard was that they had missed the boat on Christianity, and I was going to straighten them out. Though that is definitely not what I was saying, that was the picture they saw. It didn't go over well, and as a result, I learned a painful lesson in humility. For the rest of the semester, my friends ostracized me. Lesson learned. People needed to see and hear Jesus, not me.

That rejection affected me then and continues today. Sharing our faith comes with the fear of rejection, so we must learn to do our best to show Jesus' love when sharing the good news. This doesn't guarantee acceptance, but if we love them like Jesus, chances are better they'll be receptive to the message. Our witness is to be passionate about Jesus but humble in the way we present Him. The key is to keep the focus on Jesus, not ourselves. It's Jesus they need to accept, not us.

What God Sees

We worry about how we look and about being accepted, but God sees things differently when it comes to our appearance. He doesn't care if we fit in with the world; Jesus didn't. If God's concern is with outward appearance, He would choose the best-looking people to preach the gospel and draw people to Himself. But He doesn't. Look at John. God used him greatly, but he probably looked like a wild man because of the way he lived. Who is the best known of all the apostles? If you said Paul, you're correct. Paul was probably the greatest missionary who ever lived, and everywhere he went, he preached the good news about Jesus, especially to the Gentiles. He wrote letters to the various churches, and those letters make up much of the New Testament. God used him to spread the good news all over the world. What did he look like? I found this description of Paul in an apocryphal writing titled, "The Acts of Paul and Thecla." Here's the description:

> "A man small in size, bald-headed, bandy-legged, well-built, with eyebrows meeting, rather long-nosed, full of grace. For sometimes he seemed like a man, and sometimes he had the countenance of an angel." (ANF, vol. 8, p. 487)

Though not wholly negative, the physical description certainly isn't complimentary. He was short, stocky, bowlegged, bald, had a unibrow, and a long, large nose. He wasn't attractive, yet people were drawn to him. Paul's words and actions overcame his physical appearance and enabled him to be effective. He didn't have the "countenance of an angel" when he was arresting and killing Christians, but once reborn, he took on the look of his Father. His image took a backseat to the image of Christ that he reflected with passion, and that appealed to those who met him.

Paul understood he was undergoing a transformation (a transformation we undergo as well, as followers of Christ) and like John, was acutely aware of his purpose and mission (Acts 9:8-22). Paul always diverted the people's line of sight from himself to the glory of the Lord (1 Corinthians 2:1-5). He preached Jesus Christ, crucified and resurrected, with zeal and passion, never losing sight of who he was in relation to Christ. When people wanted to bow down to him, he would have none of it (Acts 14:8-15). Instead, He pointed them to Jesus — the only One deserving of their worship. With passion and humility, Paul never tired of spreading the news about Jesus, the long-awaited Messiah. He recognized the sacrifice Christ made to save him, and in return, he sacrificed himself daily to serve Him.

Knowing God used John and Paul in such powerful ways tells us that God sees beyond physical appearance. We see further evidence of this when we look at the Pharisees. If you've been a Christian for a while and read the gospels, you undoubtedly know something about them. The Pharisees were members of the ruling class of the Jews, the Sanhedrin. They commanded respect from the people and loved to be admired. Everything they did was to maintain their appearance and pious reputation. What they didn't count on was Jesus.

Jesus saw the Pharisees for who they really were, and He wasn't quiet about it. In Matthew 23:5, Jesus says, "But they do all their deeds to be noticed by men." In Matthew 23:13-28, Jesus speaks even more strongly, calling them *hypocrites*. They weren't used to being spoken to in this manner, but Jesus didn't hold back. These sections of Scripture make me think of the scene in *The Wizard of Oz* when Toto pulls back the curtain on the wizard, revealing him to be just an ordinary man. In these verses, Jesus pulls back the curtain on the Pharisees, revealing them to be "whitewashed tombs." They look good on the outside, they've spent a lot of time perfecting that image, but inside they are full of "dead men's bones." Just as God did in 1 Samuel 16, when He chose young David to be the next king of Israel, Jesus saw beyond the outward appearance of the Pharisees to their hearts. In David's case, God saw a man after His own heart; with the Pharisees, He saw men with hardened hearts of pride.

Given all we've looked at to this point, do you think God cares about the way we look? Your first inclination might be to answer *no*, He doesn't care; after all, look at John and Paul. Well, this may surprise you, but I believe God cares about our outward appearance, just not in the way we might. He doesn't care if we're dressed to the nines, adorned with jewelry, and have the latest hairstyle. Paul tells us what God cares about concerning these things in 1 Timothy 2:9-10: "I also want the women to dress modestly, with decency and propriety, adorning themselves not with elaborate hairstyles or gold or pearls or expensive clothes, but with good deeds, appropriate for women who profess to worship God" (NIV).

Some, like the Amish, take these verses literally. There is nothing wrong with that, but Paul isn't saying we should never dress up, wear jewelry, or style our hair. What he is saying is that we should not place undue emphasis on those things. We have to keep them in their proper place. Instead, he says we are to dress modestly, with decency and propriety. He puts the emphasis on living a beautiful life versus adorning ourselves with beautiful things.

In today's world, dressing modestly is a tall order. Current styles definitely lack modesty. The low-rise jeans, with barely any "rise" at all; midriff shirts; short shorts and short skirts, that leave little to the imagination; tight tops and dresses, and camisoles, which were once undergarments, are being worn as shirts. Here in the north, some schools are even allowing girls to wear sports bras with no tops over them to gym class — co-ed or not. If you think only young girls are dressing inappropriately, turn on the national news. Female anchors wear tight dresses, with low necklines and short hemlines. These immodest styles are prevalent throughout our society.

Unfortunately, some of our teenagers in the church are adopting these styles as well. They probably don't even give it a thought. Being surrounded by peers dressing like this desensitizes them to it. Still, they are not exercising good judgment based on Scripture. If you, like me, are an older woman maybe we bear some of the blame. We have a responsibility, as stated in Titus 2:3-5, to the younger women in our churches.

Though dress is not specifically mentioned in Titus, it is an area to bear in mind. Let's start with a little self-examination. Are our shorts a little too short? Our shirts a little too tight fitting? How low are our necklines? If we are to have any credibility with our young girls, we must ensure we're dressing with modesty. We may have become desensitized ourselves. So first we have to take stock of our own appearance. Are we reflecting God and His values with the way we dress?

Those of us who are mothers have a responsibility to monitor our children's dress, to make sure it is not only appropriate, but that they know the reason it matters. They need to know that God cares about how they present themselves to the world. Our children need to know the scriptures so they see in God's Word how they should live. It is our responsibility to guide them. Sometimes it is difficult and downright inconvenient, but when our kids are ready to leave for something — whether it's worship, youth group, school, or just hanging out with friends — and their dress is inappropriate, it's our job to have them change into something God will approve. It doesn't matter if it makes us late. It's too important to ignore.

Paul doesn't want us placing a lot of emphasis on our clothing and appearance, but he doesn't want us ignoring it either. God wants us to dress modestly, which can still be stylish, and then focus on being about God's business. He doesn't care about us fitting in. God cares about the way we live, what we do, and the attitude of our hearts. We must communicate this to our children with our words and our example. In doing so, we look more like our Father.

What God Calls Us to Be

We have a responsibility to be a good example to our children, but that responsibility extends to the young mothers in our churches (Titus 2:3-5). Many of the young women in our churches didn't have the benefit of an attentive, godly mother for an example. It is up to us to take them under our wings to encourage and help them as they strive to be the godly wives and mothers God calls them to be. What a privilege God has given us to pour out His love and grace on these young women while supporting and guiding them! Our encouragement can give them strength when they need it, because parenting is hard. Trust me, there is definitely a young woman, mother or not, in your congregation who will benefit from your friendship, love, and encouragement.

All you need to do is open your eyes and your heart. God will show you where you are needed.

Coming alongside a young woman in the church is a wonderful way to reflect Jesus, but there are many other ways to shine the light of Jesus in our world. I don't want to be the same woman I was the day I turned down the aisle in the grocery store to avoid being seen. From now on, I want to let Jesus' image be the one people see. I want to be more like my granddaughter, expecting rejection and persecution, but understanding it doesn't matter. Living for Jesus and sharing Him with the world is all that matters. My purpose, our purpose, is to point the way to Jesus. We can't do that if we keep letting ourselves get in the way. It's time to pull back the curtain. It's time to show them Jesus.

Bold Points to Ponder

- Read Romans 6:3-7. What did you feel when you came up out of the waters of baptism?

- Are you living intentionally for God? What do you think that looks like? (Matthew 6:33; Ephesians 5:15-17; Philippians 3:12-14)

- Share an example of passion you've experienced in your life. What were you passionate about and how did you express it?

- You are surrounded by pictures and messages of what a woman should look like. Describe a time when you fell into the "image trap."

- The desire to fit in can affect your spiritual life and witness as well. Think of a time when you kept your thoughts or beliefs to yourself. Why did you keep silent?

- Read Matthew 3:1-15. What did you see when you came upon John in the desert? Why do you think people traveled to see John?

- Who do you think people most often see and hear when with you — you or Jesus? What changes, if any, do you need to make so Jesus is front and center?

- God cares about your outward appearance being one of modesty, but He cares most about the way you live, what you do, and the attitude of your heart. In what ways can you improve on those things? (1 Timothy 2: 9-10; Hebrews 13:16; James 1:22-27)

2

Only One Name

Now that we're clear on our purpose, to be transformed more into the image of Jesus and point people to Him for salvation, we need to think about how to fulfill this purpose and what might prevent us from succeeding. Do people see Jesus in us and hear the message, or do we unwittingly throw up roadblocks to their acceptance of Him? There is a truth that will be helpful to keep in mind as you live out this life with which you are blessed. Whatever your name is, once you came up out of the water, it changed. You will forever be known by this new name, and that makes a tremendous difference. Let's talk a little about labels and names.

My best friend is one of my favorite people. We have been friends since the first grade. The community we grew up in was predominantly of Italian descent. My friend, however, was definitely not Italian. All her friends were Italian with names like Daino, Rosati, Montalto, and Picciotto. Surrounded by Italians, she felt left out because she wasn't. Over the years, she has told me she always wished she were Italian. She liked the culture, the family closeness, and the delicious food. Though she couldn't change her heritage, she did the next best thing — she married an Italian. Let me tell you, she has become the best "Italian" wife, mother, and grandmother I've ever seen. If it weren't for her hair color and skin tone, you would definitely think she's Italian. She even has the urge to feed people all the time. My friend may not be an Italian by blood, but she's "Italian."

You can tell a lot about a person by their name. For instance, in our town, if your name ended in a vowel, you probably had macaroni for dinner (pasta, for you non-Italians) every Thursday night. Just like my friend took on an Italian name and culture by marriage, we took on a new name and culture when we followed Christ. We put Him on in baptism, and when we did, we died to ourselves and to this world. We now live through Jesus and are completely new creations in Christ (2 Corinthians 5:17). As Hebrews 11:13 says, we are "foreigners and strangers on earth" (NIV). That explains why I feel so out of place sometimes. Do you ever feel that way? The truth is, we really don't belong here. Our true home is somewhere else.

Family Bonds

Before we put Christ on in baptism, we were foreigners and strangers to the kingdom of God, but now we are citizens of God's kingdom and members of His household. We may have a physical family, but we have another family as well — all the other citizens of God's kingdom — who worship together, care for each other, and support one another.

When I became a Christian, that new family was overwhelming and wonderful at the same time. It was encouraging to belong to a family of believers, who all knew the Lord and shared the same primary purpose — serving Him and one another. I remember returning to college shortly after giving my life to Christ and feeling terribly lonely. There was a fellow member of my church, a student at another college, going through the same thing. We drew strength from each other as we spoke almost daily, encouraging each other and praying together over the phone. One time, a vanload of people from my church made the three-hour drive to my school to surprise me, encourage me, and let me know I wasn't alone. That is one time my new family overwhelmed me. The love they showed a new sister in the Lord has stayed with me all these years. God uses us, if we let Him, to bless others in ways that let us know He is with us.

Being a member of God's household is a privilege, but with it comes responsibility. Let's look at this in more familiar terms. When I was growing up, my parents ingrained in me that what I did reflected on our family and our family name. In fact, my mother said something to me one night when I was in high school that has stuck with me. She said, "When you're out tonight, and any other time you leave the house, I want you to remember that you're not really alone. You have two shoulders. God is sitting on one shoulder watching you, and I'm on the other, so only do things that will make us proud." Obviously, I knew they weren't sitting on my shoulders, but just having that visual, and knowing God could see me, made me think twice on more than one occasion. I often found myself able to resist peer pressure to do things I shouldn't because of my parents' reminders. I didn't want to disappoint them, have my actions reflect poorly on them, or cause people to whisper negative things about my family.

As those who are just passing through this world, our true home is with God; our genuine family is the family of God. Our family name is "Christian." What we do reflects either positively or negatively on our family and our God. We have a choice to make. We can be like the Pharisees, putting all kinds of rules and restrictions on people but not following them ourselves, or we can be like Jesus, living by what we believe in word and deed. One turns people away; the other draws them close. Paul knew the importance of living out beliefs. He once said to the Jews, if you call yourself a Jew and talk about your relationship to God, you'd better live what you preach. If you preach that stealing is wrong, then you'd better not steal. If you preach against adultery, you must remain faithful in your marriage. Not living what you preach will cause God's name to be blasphemed among the unbelievers (Romans 2:17-24, paraphrased). Hypocrisy is a sin and has no place in a Christian's life. Paul is saying that our walk must reflect our talk; otherwise, we give God and His church, our family, a bad name. Peter puts this in a more positive light.

Knowing that we must walk the talk doesn't make it easy. Unfortunately, we often must learn things the hard way. In 1980, I was a brand-new Christian, but I knew from reading the Bible that God commands Christians not to get drunk (Ephesians 5:15-18). I was obedient to this command and never drank to excess. At that time, I enjoyed dancing, but the places available for dancing always served alcohol. One night, I went out dancing with my boyfriend, who was also a new Christian. While there, we each had one drink. We had a great time and thought nothing of it until the following Sunday. After the worship service, someone we deeply respected asked if he could speak with us. It turned out there had been a couple out dancing at the same place we were on the same night. They had been visiting the church for only a couple of weeks, but they recognized us and knew we were Christians. They saw us with drinks in hand and assumed we were drinking freely and probably getting drunk.

They had called this man and told him that our church was "just like all the rest — full of hypocrites who say one thing, but do another." That cut us to the heart. They never came back to our church. This experience weighed heavily on my heart for a long time. When they saw us, they didn't know if that was our first drink or our fifth. In their minds, Christians didn't get drunk, yet there we were with drinks in our hands. As new Christians, we had not even given a thought to how it would look to outsiders. Were they right to draw conclusions without all the facts? Of course not. But when someone is searching for the truth and a church that stands for truth, it doesn't take much to disillusion them. My actions reflected poorly on my church and my God that night, even though technically I wasn't doing anything wrong. My actions tarnished the family name.

Unwittingly, I gave that couple the wrong image of a Christian, turning them away from our congregation and, possibly, from God. I had no chance to repair the image I projected that night, but I've never forgotten them. I have prayed many times that God used someone else to reach them and bring them to a saving faith in Christ. That experience had a profound effect on me, and I've not had a drink since. Have you ever truly thought of what a serious business in which we're involved? Whatever image we present to those around us informs people's opinions about God and Christianity. What we say and do can have eternal consequences. We aren't perfect, and God doesn't expect us to be, but we must strive to live the most Christ-like lives we can. In doing so, we contribute to a positive image of God. We don't want people whispering negative things about our family — the Christian family.

Putting on the Name of Christ

Something happens to us when we take on the name "Christian." Paul writes in 2 Corinthians 5:17-20, "Therefore if anyone is in Christ, he is a new creature; the old things passed away; behold, new things have come. Now all **these** things are from God, who reconciled us to Himself through Christ and gave us the ministry of reconciliation, namely, that God was in Christ reconciling the world to Himself, not counting their trespasses against them, and He has committed to us the word of reconciliation. Therefore, we are ambassadors for Christ, as though God were making an appeal through us; we beg you on behalf of Christ, be reconciled to God." When we take on the name of Christian, we undergo a transformation and become a new person. Along with our new identity, God gives us a new, extremely important purpose.

Like Paul, so many years before us, we're entrusted with the same ministry of reconciliation and are Christ's chosen ambassadors to the world. We're His representatives, living on foreign soil, entrusted with the message of reconciliation so others can know Jesus, the One we serve, and receive eternal life. Many of us are looking for our life's purpose, but it gets no more important than this: Take His message of salvation to everyone we meet. As His ambassadors, it's vital that people see Him through us. Paul writes in 2 Corinthians 3:18, "But we all, with unveiled face, beholding as in a mirror the glory of the Lord, are being transformed into the same image from glory to glory, just as from the Lord, the Spirit." Unlike Moses, who covered his face with a veil after meeting with God until the glory of the Lord faded, our faces remain unveiled. Our faces, our lives, are to reflect the Lord's glory, and as we grow in our faith and mature, that reflected glory should keep increasing. Each time we look in the spiritual mirror, we should see less of our own image looking back at us and more of Christ's. His image is the one people should see in our lives. As one song says, "less of me and more of Him."

Take another look at 1 Peter 2:11-12. Peter gives us a lofty goal: glorify God even when we're being persecuted or experiencing trying times. Notice, he does not write "if," but makes it clear persecution and trials will happen. It's easy to look and sound like Christ when things are going our way, but when we are under stress and living through tough times, that is the genuine test. Have you ever doubted the strength of your faith? Have you ever wondered if you truly have enough faith to withstand the worst trial you can imagine? Living in the USA, we rarely experience persecution and danger because of our faith. Therefore, we may not have experienced an actual test of our faith. Some years back, I went through what was for me the most horrific thing I've experienced to date. It was definitely a test of my faith.

It was a busy day at work when I received a phone call from my father telling me there had been an accident, and my grandmother had died. My initial shock was nothing compared to what I felt when he said, "Your mother was in the car with her." He quickly explained that at the scene, it seemed she may have only broken her wrist. However, when he was following the ambulance on the way to the hospital, it stopped for a couple of minutes and then continued at a much faster pace. Because he was close to home, he turned around and went there to call me. He felt something was seriously wrong. He told me to meet him at their house (I only worked around the corner from there), so we could go to the hospital together. When we got to the hospital, I feared my dad was right. As we waited, we made calls to the rest of the family, and they joined us. I sat praying continually for God to let her live, but when the doctor came in the room, I knew from the look on his face that my prayer had not been answered as I'd wanted.

The following Sunday, just four days after losing my grandmother and mother, I went to the worship service. People were surprised to see me and asked what I was doing there. I told them the truth — I couldn't think of a better place to be. God gave me the opportunity to share my faith, amid sorrow, with the entire congregation. I thought of King David, who when after praying and fasting for the life of his son, only to lose him, got up, washed, and went into the house of the Lord and worshiped (2 Samuel 12:13-23). He lost his child, but not his faith. Yes, worship was where I needed to be and what I needed to be doing. I had lost my incredible, precious mother, but I would not lose my faith.

In the weeks and months that followed, God was my lifeline. It was my faith in Him and His plan that kept me going. In the still of the night, while my husband and children slept, I would quietly get up and go downstairs to our family room. Sitting on the sofa, wrapped in a blanket with my Bible on my lap, I would meet the Lord in the Scriptures and gather strength from knowing He was with me. It was then that I could finally rest; I was safe in His arms. Those middle of the night meetings answered my question about the reality of my faith. I had faced one of the worst trials of my life and had experienced His presence like never before. I had prayed for my mother's life to be spared, and God's answer was no. I learned that by accepting His answer and His sovereignty, we open ourselves to His comfort, His peace, and His restoration. Ultimately, when we have passed through the fire of the test, our faith emerges even stronger (James 1:2-4; 1 Peter 1:1-9).

I haven't suffered under persecution, but I have suffered the attacks of the evil one, and so have you. Thankfully, we serve a risen Lord who knows all too well the pain of suffering and persecution. Remember, people falsely accused Jesus of all kinds of things, even of getting His power from the prince of demons. They beat Him, mocked Him, and crucified Him, but He never reacted in a way to bring disgrace to the name of His Father. In fact, while being mocked, and then in the middle of His execution, He prayed for those mistreating Him. Presenting the image of Christ in our lives, living up to our family name, is more than a full-time job, it's 24/7 — through good times and bad. It isn't just something we do; it's who we *are*.

How we live sends a message about who God is to those around us. Second Corinthians 5:21 says that Christ became sin for us "so that we might become the righteousness of God in Him." Proverbs 14:34 says, "Righteousness exalts a nation." As people who are "the righteousness of God," some self-examination is in order. There are some questions we need to answer. Does the way I live exalt our nation, the kingdom of God? If image sells, are people buying into God because of what they see in me? Do my words, actions, and attitudes reflect well upon my spiritual family and my Father?

If you desire, as I do, to answer yes to these questions, and you want to have the image of Christ shine through your life and represent our family name well, there are a few things you can do. These suggestions are contrary to the world's ideas, but they line up beautifully with the Word of God.

First, realize that you are beautiful because God loves you. Satan has fooled the world, and he attempts to fool us as well, into believing our beauty is determined only by our physical characteristics. He wants us to believe that if we don't have a "plastic doll's" figure, we are worth less than the woman who does. Turn away from Satan and the world's definition of beauty, and instead seek God's definition. As a Christian, the knowledge that God loves you enough to send His Son to die for you (John 3:16) is where your self-worth should originate. In the eyes of God, you are His beautiful princess. There is a lot of talk today about self-esteem and the depression and anger resulting from low self-esteem. The problem is that most people are looking in the wrong places for their self-worth. If only people would once again believe in God and trust Him, they would know how truly special they are. Satan is the master liar (John 8:44), telling us we don't measure up. Don't fall for it. God loves you unconditionally, and even when you fall into sin and tarnish His name, He forgives you. You are, quite simply, His child; the woman He loved enough to sacrifice Jesus to save.

Second, remember in whose image God made you. Genesis 1:26-27 says, "Then God said, 'Let Us make man in Our image, according to Our likeness; and let them rule over the fish of the sea and over the birds of the sky and over the cattle and over all the earth, and over every creeping thing that creeps on the earth.' God created man in his own image, in the image of God He created him; male and female He created them." In Genesis 1, at the end of each day of creation, God "saw that it was good." After God created man in His image, God saw that "it was very good." When tempted to put yourself down because of your physical attributes or failures, remind yourself and other Christian women that you are made in the image of the one true God. God was very pleased with His creation, and that includes you.

True Worship

Paul says in Romans 12:1 that we are to offer our bodies as living sacrifices, holy and pleasing to God. He calls this our "true worship" (NIV). Before Christ and the New Covenant, the Jews were instructed to sacrifice animals in worship of God. Since Christ gave His life on the cross, there is no longer a need for animal sacrifice. Jesus gave the ultimate sacrifice. The sacrifice God now requires is for us willingly to give ourselves, our lives, over to Him and His service as worship.

Instead of berating ourselves, thinking we aren't good enough, wouldn't it be wonderful if we could thank God for the way He has made us and ask Him to make us more like Him each day? That is my heart's desire, and I hope yours as well, to reflect His glory more with each passing day and to serve Him with all my heart. It is out of love and gratitude for His sacrifice that we offer ourselves up to be used by Him for His glory daily.

One last thing, it's important to remember that being transformed into the image of Christ is a lifelong process. I have the most precious granddaughter — a true blessing from God. I'm fortunate enough to live only a few minutes from her, so I get to see her all the time. It has been such a joy to watch her change over the years. She started out as a helpless infant, and within the first two years, she transformed into a sweet little girl who could walk, talk, and give the best hugs ever. With each passing year, more of her personality, her uniqueness, shines through. She has a wonderful imagination, with many wonderful ideas of her own (some of which get her into trouble). She has a kind heart and seems to know just who needs a hug or handshake at church. That little girl brings many smiles to the wrinkled faces of the elderly that she meets. But the most wonderful thing about Julia is her love for God.

One Sunday, when Julia was about 7, the sermon was about Jesus' walking on the water and Peter's willingness to get out of the boat. Though he let the wind and waves distract him, taking his eyes off Jesus and starting to sink, Peter still got out of the boat. Julia listened intently to the sermon and then went up to our preacher after service and told him, "Mr. David, I really liked your sermon. I want to get out of the boat and walk with Jesus. I want to serve Him." Our preacher asked her why she wanted to do that and Julia replied, "Because I just love Jesus so much. I love Him more every day. I just want to serve Him and make Him happy."

The preacher said, "Is that so?" "Yes," Julia said. "I really trust Jesus, Mr. David. I trust Him more every day, and I just want to serve Him."

Julia really loves Jesus, and she understands that if she really loves Him and trusts Him, she should get out of the boat and walk with Him. She wants to be like Jesus. She wants to live like Jesus. I have much to learn from her. That little girl has the image of Jesus shining forth from her and touches the hearts of those around her. Julia has been undergoing a physical transformation since the day she was born, and she has been undergoing a spiritual transformation from the day she first started learning about Jesus.

Our transformation, like Julia's, doesn't happen overnight. It takes place a little at a time as we grow with the help of the Holy Spirit. Ephesians 4:22-24 says, "You were taught, with regard to your former way of life, to put off your old self, which is being corrupted by its deceitful desires; to be made new in the attitude of your minds; and to put on the new self, created to be like God in true righteousness and holiness" (NIV). We are created to be like God, and thankfully, even with all our faults, when God looks at us, He doesn't see them. What He sees is the woman of God we can become — a woman from whom the image of Christ brightly shines forth and reflects well on her family name — *Christian*.

Our Purpose

We can't be like the Pharisees, looking good on the outside while dead on the inside. Instead, we must strive to let the love of Jesus fill us and overflow to those we meet. Through the way we live, things we say and do, we continually point people to Jesus, where they will find unconditional love and acceptance. We have a purpose, a ministry of reconciliation, one we try to fulfill with each new day. A purpose which necessitates allowing God's glory to shine forth, rather than our own. A purpose that, as we live it out, reflects well on our spiritual family and our spiritual name.

So, the next time we check our appearance in the mirror, let's make sure it's appropriate for a woman of God.

Let's examine ourselves to see that we are reflecting the glory and love of God to the world. Just as my best friend wanted to be Italian, my prayer is that because of the way we live our lives, the people we meet will want to take on the name Christian. We know our purpose, but to fulfill it, we have to take that first step — we have to get out of the boat.

....

Bold Points to Ponder

- Names mean something. What traditions or cultural norms did you grow up with that came out of your heritage?

- Read 2 Corinthians 5:1; Hebrews 11:10-13; and Ephesians 2:19-20. What do these verses tell you about who you are and where your home is?

- Describe a time when you experienced the overwhelming love of God through His church.

- Read 1 Peter 2:11-12 and Romans 2:17-24. Reflect on these verses with the goal of pointing others to Christ.

  - How often do you think about your actions, the way you live, and the effect that has on people's opinion of God and their spiritual well-being?

  - Do you think you need to live the Christian life more intentionally and thoughtfully? If so, what will be the benefits of living that way for yourself? For others?

- Can you remember a time when your actions caused someone to "whisper negative things" about your family name of "Christian?" How did that make you feel? What, if anything, did you do about it?

- Read Exodus 34:29-35 and 2 Corinthians 3:15-18. People could tell Moses had been with God by the glow of his face, are you reflecting the Lord to others? What is your part in your transformation "into his likeness with ever-increasing glory?" (NIV)

- Describe a time when your faith was tested or stretched. How did you get through it? Did you feel the presence of God? If so, in what way?

- Time for some self-examination. (Lamentations 3:40; 2 Corinthians 13:5) Seriously consider these questions:

  - Do my words, actions, and attitudes, reflect well on my spiritual family and my Father?

  - What things do I need to change to better reflect Jesus to the world I live in?

- In a practical sense, what do you think our lives should look like if we are truly being transformed into Christ's likeness? (2 Corinthians 5:14-15; Philippians 2:1-8)

- In what way are you currently being called to step out of the boat and trust Jesus? Will you answer that call? (Isaiah 6:8; Matthew 4:18-22)

3

Love for the Word

When I was a young girl, my father wanted me to become a concert pianist. To that end, he provided me a piano, a teacher, and lots of encouragement. I never became a concert pianist, even though I wanted to please my dad. Instead, I learned that wanting something — willing it alone — will not make it happen. To be a concert pianist requires hours of daily practice, sore wrists and hands, and studying the masters to learn the theory behind the music. It requires time and sacrifice.

As Christian women, knowing our purpose of reflecting Jesus to the world is something we cannot just dream about. We need to be deeply involved and willing to sacrifice to develop the Lord's image in our lives. There's just one problem; we cannot do it on our own. Just like becoming a concert pianist, willing it to happen will not make it so. We have all tried to achieve something by sheer willpower. How many times have we made resolutions for our lives, fully intending to follow through on them, only to lose the motivation and allow them to fall by the wayside? New Year resolutions, with their high failure rates, are perfect examples. Willpower alone is not enough, but there is one thing that makes someone more likely to succeed: the buddy system. Having someone alongside us who shares the same goal definitely makes it easier to stay the course.

One of the most moving and memorable incidents recorded in Scripture is found in Matthew 14:22-33. After the feeding of the 5,000, Jesus sends the disciples off in their boat while He goes up on the mountain to pray. A storm kicks up, and the disciples are struggling against the wind and the waves. That's when it happens. The disciples see a ghostly figure, apparently walking on the water. They're terrified, but Jesus calls out to them, reassuring them it is He. Peter says in verse 28, "Lord, if it is You, command me to come to You on the water." Jesus commands him to come, and Peter gets out of the boat and begins walking on the water. Let's pick up in verse 30-32. "But seeing the wind, he became frightened, and beginning to sink, he cried out, 'Lord, save me!' Immediately, Jesus stretched out His hand and took hold of him, saying, 'You of little faith, why did you doubt?' When they got into the boat, the wind stopped."

Peter had Jesus alongside him when he got out of the boat. When Peter began to sink and yelled out for Jesus, He was right there. He saved Peter by stretching out His hand and holding onto him. The same is true for us. God does not leave us on our own to flounder. He has given us the Holy Spirit to live within us and help us as we try our best to live the Christian life. Jesus is walking with us on the rough waters of life. We need to stay close to Him, and He will stay close to us (James 4:8).

God knows us better than we know ourselves; after all, He created us. He is there to rescue us when needed, and He is intimately involved with our transformation into the image of Jesus. The Holy Spirit lives within us and guides our transformation from the inside out using God's Word as His main tool. James 1:22-25 implores us to do more than just listen to the Word. James urges us to listen to the Word and then do what it says. God's Word is alive and when implanted in our hearts, its power changes lives. As Christians who want to look like Christ in every way, having a passion for His word is essential.

Letters Home

Picture this with me. Your husband is a long way from home, and you haven't seen him for at least six months. There isn't wi-fi for your computer, nor is there cell service for your phone! He is completely "unplugged." The only way you can communicate with each other is the old-fashioned way: writing letters. One day, you're visiting with a friend when the mail arrives with a letter from your husband. You rush into the kitchen where your friend sits sipping her tea, and you hand her the letter, "Will you read this for me and tell me what it says? What it means?" Wait, a minute. Is that really what you would do with that precious letter? Of course not. It is precisely, though, what many of us do every Sunday morning. We enter the assembly and find our usual seat. We sing a few songs and then listen to a preacher tell us what the Word of God says, what it means, and how to apply it to our lives. On Wednesday night, we do the same thing. We sit in a Bible class and listen as someone speaks about the Word of God. Please don't misunderstand me. Listening to someone else speak about God's Word is a good thing, but it becomes a problem when that is our only steady diet of the Word.

Let's think about our hypothetical letter again. What would you really do with it? I know what I'd do. I'd rip it open and read every word with eagerness. I would devour each word like it was a choice morsel. How many times would you read the letter? Only once? No, if you're like me, you'd find yourself reading and re-reading that letter in the days to come. You'd dissect it, trying to read between the lines, to glean every last bit of meaning and feeling out of the words on the page. You would overflow with excitement at hearing what your husband is feeling and what is on his mind. This is what we should feel for the Word of God. The Bible is God's letter to us. We hear His voice and His heart through the Bible. We should not settle for someone else reading it and telling us what it means. We need to read it for ourselves to discover what God desires for us to know.

When I was a new Christian, I remember being in awe of God's Word. My friend Sue, another new Christian, and I would hang out in her room and just silently read our Bibles. When either of us found something especially interesting and meaningful, we would share it with each other. We found ourselves constantly interrupting each other's reading. It was amazing how God was opening our eyes to new spiritual truths with every page. I remember feeling that way all the time as a new Christian, and you probably remember that feeling, too. I couldn't wait to get by myself and read my letter from God.

Remember the passion you had for the Word when you were a new Christian. Now, think about where are you now on that passion meter. Are you filled with eagerness and excitement to hear what God desires to tell you in His Word? Do you read it with a longing to know Him and His deepest thoughts? Are you reading between the lines to discover as much meaning as you can? If not, what's happened? For a lot of us who have been Christians for several years, over time, reading the Bible became something we had to do, instead of something we couldn't wait to do. Why is that?

If we're getting low on the passion meter for reading the Bible, maybe it's because we don't fully understand the importance of it. Maybe we take it for granted. After all, the Bible is easy to acquire. We can walk in any bookstore and find plenty of Bibles choices. We can go online to order a Bible and expect it delivered to us in two days. We can even go to the app store on our phones or tablets and download a Bible with just a click. Not only do we have easy access to the Bible, but most of us own more than one. Maybe the ease with which we can get a Bible makes it seem less valuable. If we lived somewhere else — like China — and couldn't find a Bible, then maybe we would cherish it more.

Let me share with you an experience I had in 1980. The Winter Olympics were taking place in Lake Placid, New York, and I was attending the nearby State University of New York at Potsdam. As thrilled as I was to be part of the musical group performing with the late Chuck Mangione for the closing ceremonies, the clearest, brightest memory of the Olympics for me was an even bigger event!

One day, a group of us, each with a backpack filled with Bibles and tracts, got in a van and drove to Lake Placid. I spent the day approaching various athletes on the street, doing my best to greet them in their native languages and offering them a Bible. It was fascinating to see the athletes as they walked around the Olympic Village, especially the Russians. They went into any store that sold blue jeans, pointing and marveling over them. Soon, jeans were sold out all over town. My most vivid memory is of one Russian in particular. I was on the street handing out Bibles when he caught my eye from about a block away. He stared, then moved only his eyes from my face to my hand, which held a Bible, and then back again. Instinctively, I knew what he was asking, and I knew how dangerous it could be.

Each Russian athlete was accompanied by a handler whose job was to ensure the American way of life didn't entice their athlete. Defections were a reality they wanted to avoid. As the Russian drew closer, I gave a slight nod and looked straight ahead, as if beyond him. As he came alongside, I stuck out my hand, slightly, with the Bible in it. He kept looking ahead and with one smooth motion, took the Bible and pocketed it in his fur coat. He risked much by accepting it. In the Soviet Union, religion—especially Christianity—was frowned upon. Atheism was the official "religion." I often think about this man and how important it was for him to have God's Word, regardless of the consequences. He risked everything for the Bible, yet many of us take it for granted.

In His Own Hand

What makes the Bible so special? It's special because it is the very Word of God and divinely inspired. Second Timothy 3:16 says, "All scripture is God-breathed..." The scriptures come from God. We all know the story of the Ten Commandments, but let's look at it with fresh eyes. In Exodus 31:18 we read, "When the LORD finished speaking to Moses on Mount Sinai, he gave him the two tablets of the covenant law, the tablets of stone inscribed by the finger of God" (NIV). Moses had gone up on Mount Sinai and met with God. There, God wrote His words on a couple of stone tablets with His own finger. While Moses was on the mountain with God, the Israelites grew tired of waiting for his return and convinced Aaron to make a new god for them, a golden calf.

When God saw what the Israelites were doing, He wanted to destroy them all, but Moses pleaded with God for the people, and God relented. In Exodus 32:15-16, Scripture tells us, "Moses turned and went down the mountain with the two tablets of the covenant law in his hands. They were inscribed on both sides, front and back. The tablets were the work of God; the writing was the writing of God, engraved on the tablets." **Did you catch that?** God wrote His own words on those tablets and in His own hand. It strikes me as important to God that we know He was the One to write those words. Verse 16 makes it clear; it isn't up for argument — God wrote His own words of the covenant for the people to have and to read.

Let's turn back to the mountain. God agrees not to destroy the people, and Moses makes his way down the mountain. He sees for himself what the people have done — the golden calf and the worship and celebration going on, and he is furious. Remember, he is holding the precious tablets with God's words written on them. Exodus 32:19-20 shows us just how angry he is. He sees all that is going on and in anger, he does the unthinkable. He throws down the tablets, smashing them to pieces. Following the destruction of the tablets, Moses decrees a harsh punishment on the Israelites, resulting in about 3,000 deaths.

Why did Moses act so harshly? It's perhaps because the memory of God writing on the tablets, and what He wrote, was still so fresh in his mind. Exodus 20:2-3 tells us the first thing God wrote was, "I am the LORD your God, who brought you out of the land of Egypt, out of the house of slavery. You shall have no other gods before Me." **The Israelites were violating the first commandment of God.** Moses' disappointment and anger were overwhelming. He knew the Israelites needed to understand the severity of what they had done. The consequences of their sin had to be harsh enough to deter them from ever turning their backs on God again.

Moses also had to reap the consequences of his actions. In Exodus 34:1-5, we see God instructing Moses to chisel out two more stone tablets to replace the first ones he had broken. Once

Moses finishes the tablets, God tells Moses to carry them up the mountain so He can write His words on them again. Climbing the mountain isn't easy, and climbing while carrying two heavy stone tablets is even more difficult. I wonder if Moses was regretting smashing the original tablets as he climbed. What's most important here is that God wants to rewrite His words on the new tablets Himself. To God, it is essential that His people have His words, written with His own hand.

His desire for His people to have His Word extends beyond the tablets of the covenant. In Jeremiah 36:1-2 we read, "In the fourth year of Jehoiakim the son of Josiah, king of Judah, this word came to Jeremiah from the LORD, saying, 'Take a scroll and write on it all the words which I have spoken to you concerning Israel and concerning Judah, and concerning all the nations, from the day I first spoke to you, from the days of Josiah, even to this day.'" Here, we see God instructing Jeremiah to write down His words. When God wrote on the tablets of stone back in Exodus, it was somewhere around 1440 B.C. Now we see Him in Jeremiah, again concerned with His words being written, and this is somewhere around 605 B.C. Over 800 years have passed between these two events, but God's desire to have His Word written down for the people has not changed. Jeremiah was a prophet, and in 2 Peter 1:20-21, Peter makes it clear that the words spoken by a prophet were the words of God. God's people have always understood that the scriptures they had were the words of God.

Bible Beginnings

We know that Scripture says God is the same yesterday, today, and tomorrow. This maxim applies to His Word as well. Let's look at Revelation 14:13. "And I heard a voice from heaven saying, 'Write, Blessed are the dead who die in the Lord from now on!'" John wrote this around 95 A.D. Again, God is commanding one of His people to write down His words. This is about 700 years after the example in Jeremiah. God truly never changes. He still wants His people to know that His words are written for them, by His own hand, and by the Spirit of God through men of His choosing. All Scripture truly is God-breathed.

Writing this chapter brought back another memory from when I first became a Christian. I was so excited about my new faith that I wanted to share it with my boyfriend. At first, he was a bit worried I'd joined a cult, but I encouraged him to read the Bible to learn about Jesus and discover what God wanted for his life. Many nights, he'd pick me up, and we'd drive to an empty parking lot, park under a streetlight, and study the Bible. (No smartphones with flashlights back then!) We had a real hunger for the Word.

One night, as we were deep in study, there was a knock on the car window, followed by a flashlight in our faces. Mark rolled down the window, and the policeman asked us what we were doing. Boy, was he surprised when we told him we were studying the Bible and held up our Bibles to prove it! He still told us we needed to move along, but I think I heard him say as he walked away, "Now, I've seen everything."

You may wonder why we had to sit in his car to study the Bible. His parents would've been upset if they knew he was reading it. At home, he hid the Bible behind a college textbook so they'd think he was studying for school instead of for eternal life. He'd been raised in a faith tradition that taught only the ordained could understand Scripture, which made it hard for him to be open about reading it. But that didn't last long—when you truly love God and His Word, you can't help but share it.

Have any of my memories brought up any for you? Have you remembered the passion and excitement you had for reading and studying God's Word when you first gave your life to Christ?

The wonder that dawned on you as your eyes were opened to each new spiritual truth? God puts such a high premium on communicating with us that He wrote the words Himself and later, through the inspiration of the Holy Spirit, wrote His Word through men of His choosing. How can that not excite us? The Creator of the universe wants to speak with each one of us.

When you started reading this chapter, was reading the Bible something you needed to check off your to-do list? Were you pretty low on your passion meter? I hope the needle on your passion meter is moving closer to "Wow!" God has something to tell each one of us, to reveal to us every time we open the Bible. God speaks; let's listen.

Bold Points to Ponder

- Share a time when having someone alongside you with the same goal helped you to stick with and succeed.

- Read Jeremiah 15:16 and Psalm 119:103-104. Is that the passion you have for the Word of God? If not, what steps can you take to move yourself closer to that kind of love for the Word?

  - Think of someone you know who had/has that passion for the Word. How does it show in her life?

- Describe the way you felt when you first began reading the Bible as a new Christian

  - Think about how you feel about reading God's Word today. Has your excitement and eagerness to be in the Word waned over the years? If so, why do you think that is? If not, what keeps it fresh for you?

- Read Exodus 31:18 and 32:15-16. How do you feel about the fact that God wrote His Word with His own finger on the tablets of stone? Why do you think it was so important to God that we know He had written on the tablets Himself?

- Why is it important that we read the Bible and study it for ourselves? (Psalm 119:33-38)

- Have you gone through periods when you were not reading the Word? If so, what effect would you say it had on your life? When in a period of consistent reading and studying of the Word, what effect did it have on your life?

- Read 2 Timothy 2:15. What does it mean to "accurately handle the word of truth?" How does this fit in with our purpose as discussed in Chapters 1 and 2?

- Write something the Holy Spirit has shown you in God's Word this past week? Why do you think He revealed that to you? How will you apply it in your life?

- If you find yourself lacking a passion to study the Word and apply it to your life, what are some ways you can rekindle or develop a desire to read and study the Bible?

4

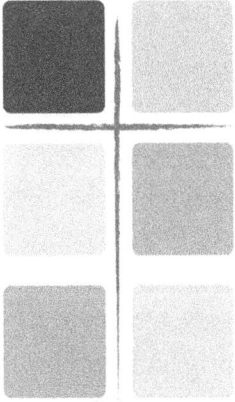

Deemed Worthy

It was a beautiful March day in Syracuse, New York, in 1993. Running errands without a coat made it feel like spring was finally coming. Upon arriving home, I opened a window, turned on the radio, and began cleaning the house. Suddenly, an announcement on the radio caught my attention — blizzard warning! That warning must be for some other state, I thought to myself. I was wrong. My husband called, and I told him I was getting ready to go to the grocery store because we were almost completely out of the staples — bread, milk, and eggs — and I wanted to get them before the storm. He laughed at me, saying there was no way a blizzard was coming. I went to the store anyway because we needed those things. The first flakes began falling around 5:30 PM. By 6:30 PM, there was enough snow that we took the children out to play in it and pulled them on the sled. The next morning, 43 inches of snow blanketed the ground. Everyone was glad I'd gotten groceries; we were prepared for the storm.

For the Christian, God's Word is the number one staple of our spiritual diet. We know we need it, but for many, instead of it being a priority, reading the Bible is something we fit into our schedule if we have time. Ignoring the Word eventually leads to spiritual death. Why is that? What makes it so powerful? Think back to my Russian athlete in the previous chapter. He risked everything to have a Bible. He probably heard whisperings about the Bible in his country. I'm sure he saw athletes praying before competing and wondered why they built their lives around this book. Maybe it made him curious, or maybe he wanted to believe and truly hoped this book was as powerful as he'd heard. It could be he hoped God was reaching out to humanity. Maybe that hope caused him to reach out for the Bible in my hand.

Some countries have outlawed Christianity or the Bible. They imprison people caught reading and teaching the Bible or worshiping Christ. We are fortunate in the United States not to suffer that kind of persecution. We freely attend worship and read our Bibles out in the open. Though anger aimed at Christians has risen in recent years, we don't suffer the way others do. In the case of my Russian friend, his government continually maligned the Bible. They tried to destroy all the Bibles and made it against the law to read it. The Soviet Union did not allow Bible shipments into the country. Fortunately, all their attempts failed thanks to brave men and women who risked everything smuggling Bibles into the country. No matter what the government did, they could not eliminate God's Word from their society. They limited the physical copies of the Bible, but people who had one shared it with others. They could not remove God's Word from the hearts and minds of the people.

There was a spiritual hunger in that atheistic country. What the government didn't understand is that God's Word is eternal. Matthew 24:35 says, "Heaven and earth will pass away, but My words will not pass away." They were fighting a losing battle. Everything will pass away, and the Soviet Union did, but God's Word is eternal. Thankfully, in 1989, the Cold War ended, and gradually, with the Bible allowed into the country, churches began springing up. God's Word survived the barrenness of Soviet Russia, and it continues to save and inspire people in other countries where it is banned. God's Word is here to stay.

That was the Soviet Union; that could never happen here. Are you sure? Atheism is on the rise in the United States, and politicians and other groups have been systematically trying to remove God from the public square. With atheism becoming more popular, many people try to prove that God's Word is nothing more than a book written by men. In fact, a number of scientists have set out to prove that the Bible isn't true and God doesn't exist, but end up becoming believers themselves. John Clayton is one such scientist.

Mr. Clayton was a devout atheist and scientist. He set out to write a book titled *All the Stupidity of the Bible*. What he didn't expect was that as he researched, studied, and wrote this book to prove to everyone that God is made up and Christianity is "stupid," he would come face to face with science that instead proved God's existence. Being unable to deny what he found, John put on Christ in baptism and turned his back on atheism. He now has a thriving ministry called "Does God Exist?" in which he reaches out to young and old through the internet and personal appearances with the message that yes, God exists, and He wants a relationship with you. He teaches others what he found — that God and science are not at odds with each other, God and people are. Mr. Clayton teaches how Jesus bridges that distance between man and God.

The perfection of God's Word and the importance He placed on writing it encourages us to take a careful look at it. Second Timothy 2:15 says, "Be diligent to present yourself approved to God as a workman who does not need to be ashamed, accurately handling the word of truth." The word *diligent* implies effort or hard work, and in the Greek, it means to exert one's self, to be zealous. God wants us to do more than just read the Bible. He wants us to be zealous in our study of it. He wants us to put time and energy into understanding it and applying it. All Christians should want to read and study God's Word, because by it, we learn who God is, who we are in His eyes, and what we need to change to be more like Christ. Becoming who God designed us to be in Christ is worth the time, effort, and sacrifice needed to put into knowing His Word.

In the verse above, Paul provides us with another reason for studying the Bible: being able to accurately handle the Word of Truth. Remember our purpose — to point others to Jesus. That involves sharing the Bible with them and teaching them what it says about Jesus. To be successful at that, we must study the Word ourselves. Understanding what the Bible says and how different verses fit together gives us a full picture of who God is, who Christ is, why He came, and what that means for each one of us. With that knowledge, we can teach others about God and His plan to save them. It takes time and effort to fit the pieces of Scripture together, but it is worth it, both for us and for those we teach about Jesus.

One day, a friend asked me, "Why do you spend so much time reading the Bible over and over? I've read it through cover to cover. There's no need to read it again." He doesn't realize what the Bible is. If we treat the Bible like any other book, then he's right, we need not read it more than once. When I read a fiction book, I rarely read it again. But the Bible isn't like any other book. It isn't a collection of fictional stories that once you've read them, there is nothing more to glean from reading them again. This book is unique. The Bible has the power to change lives, and the more we study it, the more we change.

Under Construction

God is in the transformation through renovation business, and the Bible is His primary tool. It tears down areas in our lives that aren't in harmony with Him and rebuilds them in such a way as to transform who we are. Gratefully, God deems us worthy. Hebrews 4:12 says, "For the word of God is living and active and sharper than any two-edged sword, and piercing as far as the division of soul and spirit, of both joints and marrow, and able to judge the thoughts and intentions of the heart." **God's Word is alive. Let that sink in.** Because it is alive, each time we read it, we learn something new. It's just like when you spend time with a friend. Each time you get together, you talk and either affirm something you already knew, or you learn something new about them. Each time we read the Bible, it affirms our belief or opens our eyes to something we've never seen before. The Word of God continually teaches us and changes our hearts. Spending time in the Bible allows God's Word to continue the renovation in our lives begun on the day we became a Christian. Transformation requires that we allow the Holy Spirit to teach us and change our hearts through God's Word. Each time we open the Bible, we open the door to God lovingly molding us into a better representation of His Son.

God had reasons for writing His Word. I'm sure you've played "Telephone" before. You know what happens as each person passes along a message to the next. By the end, the message turns out to be something completely different.

Everyone has a great laugh about it. Passing along God's Word in that way, however, would be no laughing matter. God commanded His people to talk about Him and what He's done as they raised their children, but He knew that passing down His Word orally alone would be like playing "Telephone." He wants us to have an accurate accounting of who He is, what He did and why throughout history. He wants us to know how to become His children and live with Him eternally. God took no chances. Writing His Word preserved its accuracy. God chose the written word to communicate with us, so we can know the Truth.

Another reason the Word of God was written is to prove the divinity of Jesus Christ. John 20:30-31 says, "Therefore many other signs Jesus also performed in the presence of the disciples, which are not written in this book; but these have been written so that you may believe that Jesus is the Christ, the Son of God; and that believing you may have life in His name." When we take the Scriptures as a whole, they prove Jesus' divinity. Recently, I was speaking with a Jewish man and the question of what matters most to me came up. I shared with him that my faith and living in a way that pleases Christ are the most important things to me. To my surprise, he expressed that he feels the same. He said that as a Jew, he was raised on the Old Testament but began reading the New Testament as an adult. He said in reading the New Testament, he realized he'd been told only half of the story. Now he understands the full story, believes that Jesus is the Messiah, and has given his life to Christ. He now lives to reflect Christ to others, all because he read *both* the Old Testament and the New Testament.

Revisit the Past

How did this happen? There are many prophecies in the Old Testament concerning the Messiah, and the New Testament shows Jesus fulfilling them. The Scriptures testify to who Jesus is. In Acts 18:28, we see Apollos, after being taught by Priscilla and Aquila, debating the Jews and *proving from Scripture* that Jesus was the Christ. He wasn't the only one — Jesus Himself did the same thing. Look at Luke 24. Jesus, after the resurrection, is walking along the road with two of His disciples, and according to verse 27, He uses Scripture, beginning with Moses and the prophets, to teach them about Himself. We can see the same thing happening in Acts 8. Philip preaches Jesus to an Ethiopian eunuch, beginning with Isaiah 53:7.

How many of us could do that today? Do we know the Old Testament well enough to use it to prove who Jesus is? Someone might say, "But we're New Testament Christians." Yes, we are, but we find our heritage in the Old Testament. God tells His story from Genesis to Revelation, not just from Matthew to Revelation. To ignore the Old Testament is to ignore the story of why Jesus needed to come to earth. The Old Testament brings a richness and understanding of things in the New Testament that we would otherwise miss. For instance, understanding the Passover and the sacrifice of the Passover lamb leads to a greater understanding of Jesus' sacrifice and the meaning of the shedding of His blood. Studying and understanding the Old Testament strengthens our faith and gives us a powerful tool to use when teaching others about Jesus.

All that study of Scripture fulfills another purpose God had for writing His Word — to give humanity hope. Romans 15:4 says, "For whatever was written in earlier times was written for our instruction, so that through **perseverance and the encouragement of the Scriptures** we might have hope" (emphasis added). When I was in college, I met a young woman who felt hopeless. She was depressed, felt like she would never make it through school, had no friends, and felt worthless. As we spent time together,

I began telling her about Jesus and what He did so she could have hope — the hope of eternal life. Gradually, as I showed her in Scripture how Jesus loved the loveless, healed the sick, and befriended the friendless, she had flickers of hope. After some time, she was buried with Christ in baptism, and I was privileged to watch this caterpillar of a young woman turn into a beautiful butterfly full of faith in Christ.

We live in a world filled with hopeless people. In our own country, the richest country in the world, we have many people without hope, as evidenced by the rising suicide rate. God knew we would all have trouble in this life. He knew there were a variety of experiences and circumstances that could rob us of hope. So, He did something about it. He wrote of people like Job, who lost everything and whose circumstances were beyond horrible, to show us that with faith, there is always hope. He wrote about the Israelites in bondage for 450 years, who never lost hope because they had faith in the One True God and His ability to save them. Throughout Scripture, God's people hold onto faith and hope through times of trial, persecution, and even face death because they know God will never leave them. God wanted us to know that we are never without hope if we put our faith in Him. Using God's Word, we can teach others about the hope offered through Jesus and remind ourselves of that hope as well. When feeling down or discouraged, instead of dwelling on that, open up God's Word, and read it with an open heart. His Word will renew your hope.

Along with hope, God's Word is a warning. First Corinthians 10:11 says, "These things happened to them as examples and were written down as **warnings for us**, on whom the culmination of the ages has come" (NIV; emphasis added). The Bible contains many examples of people disobeying God and what happened to them, all to serve as warnings to us today. There is one account that serves to warn us to never stop reading the Bible. Take a trip back with me to about 640 BC, and read about a king of Judah named Josiah. We find his story in 2 Kings 22:1-23:3. Go ahead. Take some time to read it. When you get back, we'll talk about it.

So, what did you think? This story amazes me and even scares me a little. In 2 Kings 22:2, we find out some things about Josiah. Josiah was a good king who followed the Lord. He started purging Judah and Jerusalem of the pagan idols when he was 12 years into his rule. Following the ways of David and purifying the land of pagan influences, sounds great. Then we find out something amazing: After he's been king for 18 years, he sends his secretary with a message to the temple, which is being repaired. While there, the high priest tells the secretary, "I have found the book of the law in the house of the LORD" (22:8). On the surface, this sounds like a great thing; they've found the book of the law. Here's the question that bothers me: Why was it lost in the first place?

Josiah followed two of the most wicked kings in Israel's history — Manasseh, his grandfather, and Amon, his father. Though we don't know exactly when the book of the law went missing, we know that Manasseh and Amon were not following God's laws. More than that, they did not abide by what was written in Deuteronomy 17:18 - 19. When a king took the throne, he was supposed to write himself a copy of the law and read it continually so he would fear the Lord and follow the law closely. Apparently, Josiah's predecessors didn't do this. Shaphan, the secretary, reads the Book of the Law. He understands the importance of it and goes to see Josiah. He tells him, "Hilkiah the priest has given me a book" (22:10). Then he reads it to the king.

Josiah's reaction is strong and immediate. He understands the significance and realizes he and the people have broken the covenant with the Lord. He tears his robes and sends his trusted advisers to "inquire of the LORD" (22:13) about what's written in the book. Josiah knows God is angry at Judah for not obeying the Word. Josiah is full of shock and anguish because he discovers that his "fathers" and dare I say, Josiah himself, have not lived as the book of the law commanded. He thought he had been living the way God wanted him to live, and in many ways, he was, but after hearing the Word of God, he realized he wasn't living according to the covenant. He calls all the people together and reads the book of the law to them. Then Josiah and the people renew the covenant with the Lord to "walk after the LORD, and to and keep His commandments and His testimonies and His statutes with all his heart and all his soul, to carry out the words of this covenant that were written in this book" (23:3).

Why didn't Josiah know he wasn't living as God would have him live? Didn't he understand they had desecrated the temple with the things of pagan religions? Why didn't he know that the people and priests should not be worshiping on the "high places?" Because Josiah did not know the Word of God. "There is a way which seems right to a man, but its end is the way of death" (Proverbs 14:12). Josiah thought he was following God. He thought he was doing right, only to find out from God's Word that he had broken that covenant.

Know the Way

Like Josiah, we may think we are living a godly life; we may think we are following God's will, but if we don't know His Word, how can we be sure that the way that seems right to us is not a path of separation from God? God chooses His words carefully. He says exactly what He means. It is not an accident that He tells us to love Him with all our heart, all our soul, all our strength, and all our mind. God wants our minds engaged.

He wants us intellectually involved in our relationship with Him through the study of His Word. Romans 12:2 says for us to be transformed by the renewing of our minds. God doesn't want pre-programmed robots. He wants people who choose to follow Him and put in the time and effort to get to know Him by studying His Word.

King Josiah's story serves as a stern warning for us of what can happen when we stray from the Word of God. The distance between God and His people grew gradually. By the time Josiah finally read God's Word, things were terrible. Second Kings 23:6 says, "He took the Asherah pole from the temple of the LORD to the Kidron Valley outside Jerusalem and burned it there" (NIV). It's hard to believe an Asherah pole was actually in the temple of the Lord. If we don't stay in the Word and have a passion for not only knowing the Word of God, but living in obedience to it, we put ourselves in danger of one day finding "Asherah poles" in our own lives that we never even realized we built.

Once Josiah read the Word of God, he was filled with a passion to know it, share it, and live by it. Do you remember having that kind of passion when you first started reading the Bible? We need the determination to know and live by the Word because His Word protects us from being deceived by false teachers, false philosophies, or teachers just in error. In Acts 17:11, Luke praises the Bereans for checking what Paul was preaching against the Scriptures to be sure he spoke the truth. This is good practice for us to have. If what Paul said was compared with the Scriptures, what any of us teach should be as well. Preachers and teachers make mistakes. Without the plumb line of Scripture, it would be easy to be misled. If what we hear, think, or desire does not line up with Scripture, it cannot be right.

False teachings and philosophies bombard us daily. You can probably name some. The first one that pops into my mind is,

"If it feels good, do it." Satan's great at making something bad sound good. He's the original "spinner." His twisting of God's Word began way back in Genesis 3:1 when he asked Eve, "Indeed, has God said, 'You shall not eat from any tree of the garden'?" He put just enough truth into his question to make it sound right. Satan hasn't changed. He still uses the same bag of tricks he used in the Garden of Eden. We need to recognize Satan's lies; the Bible helps us do that.

Look what Paul writes about this in Colossians 2:8. "See to it that no one takes you captive through philosophy and empty deception, according to the tradition of men, according to the elementary principles of the world, rather than according to Christ." We live in a secular, humanistic society. Paul could have been writing these very words today, so be on guard. Don't get taken in. Know God's Word so that you can discern truth from lies. The light of God's Word removes all the disguises with which Satan dresses up his lies, so we can see the truth. Studying the Bible and knowing what it says prevents us from being led astray.

The Word of God instructs us how to live pure lives for Christ. People laughingly say that babies don't come with instruction manuals. Our God is awesome because He knew, as His children, we needed an instruction manual for life. He knew the philosophies and standards of the world would be continually swirling around us and would cause confusion unless we had the truth of His Word to guide us. Psalm 1:1-2 says, "How blessed is the man who does not walk in the counsel of the wicked, nor stand in the path of sinners, nor sit in the seat of scoffers! But his delight is in the law of the LORD, and in His law he meditates day and night." The wickedness of the world surrounds us. We hear the words of the mockers and scoffers of Christ daily. How do we make sure we don't become one with the world? We delight in God's Word, and we meditate on it day and night. Psalm 119:9 asks, "How can a young man keep his way pure? By keeping it according to Your word" (NIV). And in verse 105, we read, "Your word is a lamp to my feet and a light to my path." God's Word tells us how to live a pure life as a Christian. His Word lights our way like a flashlight at night, but we have to turn it on. We have to use it. It is up to us to be obedient to God's Word.

God, our Father, was passionate about writing down His Word for us, and we should be equally eager to read it, study it, and apply it to the way we live. It is God's love letter to each of us. Let's read it as it was meant to be read — with a desire and passion to know the One who wrote it. In approaching God's Word like this, the words of life it contains and the truth it embodies, renovate our lives and transform us with each passing day. God's Word is the staple of our spiritual lives. With it, we are ready for anything.

Bold Points to Ponder

- We all know what the "staples" are when it comes to groceries. What do you consider to be the staples of your life as a Christian?

- Read Mark 13:31. What does this verse mean to you?

  - Do you draw reassurance from it? If so, in what way?

- Read 2 Timothy 2:15. Are you zealous for God's Word? Describe.

  - How much of your desire for the Word is focused on reading? How much is focused on study?

◆ What is the difference between reading the Word and studying the Word?

- We meet many people who do not believe the Bible is the Word of God. If you were in a position to share the Word of God with someone who did not believe in the infallibility of the Word, how would you go about doing so?

- Read Deuteronomy 4:2 and Revelation 22:18-19. What does this tell you about how God views accuracy of His Word?

- Read Luke 18:13-27 and Acts 8:25-40. Where do you rate your knowledge of the Old Testament? Give yourself a number rating from 0 to 10, with 0 being *"I don't know anything about it"* and 10 being *"Just call me a scholar!"*

  ◆ Do you see the importance of knowing more of the Old Testament? What are some ways you can learn more about it?

- What is one of your favorite scriptures to read when you need to refresh your hope?

  ◆ Read Isaiah 40:29-31. What are the effects of hope in the Lord?

- What can you do this week to prepare for any impending spiritual storm and what are some tools you can use to help with your study of the Bible?

5

... Lost No More

It began like any other summer day — windows open, music playing, and my Sheltie dog, Scotty, out in the yard chasing squirrels. With the warm breeze came the sound of Scotty's barking through the open windows. Some time passed, and I realized I no longer heard him. I looked out the back window and saw the fence between my house and my neighbor's was missing — and so was my dog. My neighbor, who'd been in a dispute with me and others whose property bordered his, had removed the fence without warning. I dropped everything, threw on my shoes, grabbed his leash, and ran out the door. Alternately running and walking, I searched the neighborhood, calling his name as I looked for him. My dog was lost, and I wasn't going home without him. Eventually, I found him. Joy and relief filled my heart as I hugged him, petted him, and led him home.

Picture this with me. A friend of yours recently moved, and you're on your way to her new house for the first time. You're driving along, singing with the radio, and enjoying the trip. She told you it would take about 20 minutes to get there. Now you've been driving for about 25 minutes and are looking carefully at your surroundings. You're sure you must be almost there. Thirty minutes come and go, and you're getting a little anxious. You're thinking, *Did I miss a turn?* But you keep on driving. After 40 minutes, you admit to yourself that you're lost. Unfortunately, it's now dark, and you're getting a little panicked about being lost in the middle of nowhere with no cell service.

You pull over on the side of the road hoping to figure out which way to go. Suddenly, you see headlights in your rearview mirror. The car pulls over, stopping directly behind you. That anxiety has just ratcheted up to fear. Who is that behind you? What do they want? With their headlights on, you can't tell who it is, but you can see whoever it is has gotten out of the car and is approaching you. You lock the doors and fumble with the key in the ignition to start the car. You're just about to pull away when the person reaches your door and peers in the window. It's your friend. Relief floods through you as you park the car and lower the window. She explains she became worried about you when it got so late, and she went out to look for you. You thank her for caring about you and gratefully follow her home.

Can you relate to this story? We have all been lost before. In fact, we have all been lost spiritually at one time, unknowingly taking the wrong road, singing along the way. Thankfully, God loves us enough to come looking for us and get us back on the right road. That's what He did for Saul. He was on the wrong road, actively working against God by rounding up the followers of Jesus for punishment. Saul didn't know it, but he was lost. Jesus saw Saul, knew what he was doing, recognized that he was lost, and came looking for him. Paul, the name Saul is more commonly known by, talks about the day Jesus found him in Acts 22:3-16. He starts out by talking about the wrong road he was on when Jesus found him and the new road Jesus put him on — the right road. Saul met Jesus while lost on the wrong road and because Jesus found him, he gained a new mission and purpose that reverberates through the world still today.

He Leaves the 99 for the One

If there is one thing we know about God, it's that He cares deeply for the lost. Second Peter 3:9 says, "The Lord is not slow about His promise, as some count slowness, but is patient toward you, not wishing for any to perish but for all to come to repentance." God loves us and wants everyone to repent and turn to Him. He wants everyone to be saved. He actively seeks out those who are lost to bring them to Him. In Ezekiel 34:15-16, we read, "I myself will tend my sheep and have them lie down, declares the Sovereign LORD. I will search for the lost and bring back the strays. I will bind up the injured and strengthen the we.Our God is an active God. He loves His people enough to go out in search of them when they are lost and lead them home.

Who are the lost? Simply put, the lost are those who do not know Jesus Christ as Lord and Savior. They are all those on the broad road that leads to destruction and who will be eternally condemned to hell if they do not choose to follow Christ. We were all lost at one time, living without Jesus and following our own desires and paths. Praise God that He didn't leave us this way. Christ found us and completely changed our lives. When we speak of the lost, do we feel in our hearts what God feels when He sees them and thinks about them? I would like to think so, but I have noticed different attitudes in the church toward the lost of which to be aware.

The first of those attitudes is a general talking down about the lost. We talk about the "world" and how it is so far off the mark of what God teaches. We sound almost arrogant when we talk about the state of the world. The world is full of sin! We sound so surprised and horrified by that. It shouldn't surprise us, because without God, of course, the world is full of sin. The people in the world belong to the prince of this world — Satan. They are slaves to sin and are doing what comes naturally to those who follow the father of lies. The lost don't know the way, the truth, and the life. It is interesting to me that we often get more worked up about the sin in the world, sin that is to be expected, than about the sin in our own lives and in the church. We know the Lord and have chosen a life as slaves to righteousness, and when we sin, we go against the way we should be living in light of God's grace. When we harbor sin in our lives, we are just as lost as those in the world — maybe more so — because we know the Truth.

Have Perspective

While being aware of the sin in the world, we must also face our own sin with eyes wide open. Facing our sin should cause us sorrow because our sin hurts God. That sorrow should lead us to repentance and once more living according to God's Word and will (2 Corinthians 7:8-10). Jesus warned us against focusing on someone else's sin while neglecting our own (Luke 6:41-42). At the least, we will be ineffective in reaching others; at the worst, we will turn people away from God. We are in no place to be putting down the world for its sin when we have our own problems with sin. Are we better than they are? No. We are just blessed to have the forgiveness found in Christ. What *should* upset us about the world is not the sin we see there, but the lost people who populate it. God's heart breaks over the lost souls in the world, and our hearts should break as well. Let's be sure our focus is on the people, not the sin.

Another attitude that concerns me is a "political correctness" that is finding its way into the church. In society, there is the unspoken rule that we must not say or do anything that might offend someone. That is difficult to do when it seems people are just looking to feel offended. Unfortunately, that idea is making its way into the church. So, we change what we call things to make them sound more acceptable and less offensive. For instance, we are quick to find and label sin in the world, but when we talk about ourselves and others in the church, do we call it sin?? How often is sin actually talked about in our pulpits today? Instead, we call sin a "mistake." It's less upsetting this way. It is easier for me to admit to making a mistake than to committing a sin. We need to call it what it is, sin, and feel broken-hearted over it. We are too easy on ourselves. Jesus, in the Sermon on the Mount, said, "Blessed are those who mourn" (Matthew 5:4). We must mourn over our sin, repent of it, and ask forgiveness. It is sin, ungodliness, not a mistake.

Political correctness has also crept into what we call people who do not yet belong to Christ. When I first became a Christian, people who were not Christians were called non-Christians. Somewhere along the way, someone decided that sounds too harsh and exclusive, so the term *unchurched* has found its way into the vocabulary of the church. Supposedly, this term is less likely to offend people or cause them to feel excluded. There are a couple of problems with the term *unchurched*. Churches use the term without knowing what it means. The Barna research group conducted a survey of unchurched people, and it might surprise you to find out that one out of every five unchurched adults are born-again Christians. Only about four percent of those have a biblical worldview. These people are not "unchurched"; they are lost. The term *unchurched* can describe any adult who has not attended a Christian church service in the last six months. When we use the term *unchurched*, do we know what it means, or are we just speaking "Christianese" again? Jesus said He came to seek and save the lost, not the unchurched. Jesus said you are for Him or against Him (Matthew 12:30). There is no middle ground. Either someone is saved, or they are lost. Either they are a Christian, or they are not. We have to be careful not to allow the world's idea of political correctness to infiltrate our congregations or our thinking. The Word of God must influence our thinking; that is where we find truth.

My other problem with the politically correct term *unchurched* is the effect it can have on those of us in the church. *Unchurched* holds less emotion and sense of urgency than "the lost." If someone is unchurched, if they haven't attended a Christian worship service in the last six months; that does not seem near as urgent a situation as someone who is lost. They are both on the same road to hell, but one condition sounds less grave than the other. We must not allow ourselves to become complacent about those who do not know Christ.

God certainly understands the urgency to have the lost come to know Him. In Acts, 8, we read about Philip and the Ethiopian eunuch. Philip is told by an angel to go to a desert road between Jerusalem and Gaza. Philip goes and meets the eunuch on the way. He is traveling home from Jerusalem in a chariot and reading the book of Isaiah. Philip, again told by an angel, runs up to the chariot and runs alongside it. When he hears the man reading Isaiah, he asks him if he understands it. The eunuch says he needs someone to explain it to him and invites Philip into the chariot. The eunuch was reading this passage of Scripture: "He was led like a sheep to the slaughter, and as a lamb before its shearer is silent, so he did not open his mouth. In his humiliation he was deprived of justice. Who can speak of his descendants? For his life was taken from the earth" (Acts 8:32-33, NIV). **Philip started there, with that Scripture (Isaiah 53:7-8), and told him all about Jesus and salvation through Him. Acts 8:36-39 continues,** "As they traveled along the road, they came to some water and the eunuch said, "Look, here is water. Why shouldn't I be baptized? And he gave orders to stop the chariot. Then both Philip and the eunuch went down into the water and Philip baptized him. When they came up out of the water, the Spirit of the Lord suddenly took Philip away, and the eunuch did not see him again, but went on his way rejoicing" (NIV).

God sent Philip to where the eunuch was traveling for a purpose. The eunuch was a lost soul, searching the Scriptures, and in need of hearing the gospel. God wanted him to be saved, so He sent Philip to him to explain the gospel and save his soul. I can relate with the eunuch. I'll tell you more about my conversion later, but like the eunuch, I was searching. God saw my searching and brought a most unlikely person into my life to show me the way of salvation. He saw my need and reached out to me through one of His children. He seeks the lost to bring them home to Him and uses us, His children, to reach them. We know this was Philip's mission on that road, because as soon as he baptized the eunuch into Christ, the Spirit of the Lord took Philip away and set him down in Azotus. Philip had completed his mission on the road to Gaza, and God brought him to the next place he needed to be.

On a little side note, notice the angel doesn't tell Philip *why* he is to go to the road leading from Jerusalem to Gaza. He just tells him to go, so Philip goes. Once on the road, he hears the angel instructing him to get near the chariot. Again, he obeys. Philip hears him reading and asks him if he understands what he is reading. From that simple question, Philip shares the gospel with the eunuch and brings him to a saving faith in Jesus. I need to be more like Philip, and perhaps you do, too. Our ears and eyes must stay open to the opportunities God puts in front of us to share the good news about Jesus Christ. He has people He wants us to notice and teach about Jesus. This requires us to take our focus off ourselves and actively look for where God wants to use us each day.

God Can Use Us Anywhere

No matter where we find ourselves and no matter where we live, God can use us. Right now, you are where God wants you to be. There is no such thing as coincidence. God knows where you are, where you live, and where you are needed — He put you there. Like Philip, we have a mission field. God put Philip on that road to reach the Ethiopian eunuch. He has put us in our respective towns to reach people there. You've likely heard the phrase, "Bloom where you're planted." Just remember, that doesn't mean that God won't uproot you and replant you in another location where you are needed — just like He did with Philip. Wherever God has planted you, though, He wants you to have open eyes and ears to hear the need of a lost soul you might meet. We must all remain open to the leading of the Holy Spirit and feel the urgency of saving the lost. When He calls us, or sends us, our answer should be like Philip's, an immediate *yes*.

Jesus has a sense of urgency and heart for the lost. In John 8, the teachers of the law and the Pharisees tried to trap Him once again. They brought a woman caught committing adultery before Him. They reminded Him that Moses commanded that a woman caught in adultery should be stoned. Then they inquired, "What then do you say?" (John 8:5). Jesus didn't respond. Instead, He bent down and began writing on the ground. Here again, we see God writing with His own finger as He did when He wrote the Ten Commandments on the stone tablets. Many have tried to imagine what Jesus wrote on the ground. Could He have been writing the Ten Commandments? Considering what happens next, it is as good a theory as any. They kept questioning Him, wanting an answer they could use to accuse Him. Instead of answering their question, Jesus told them that if any of them were without sin, he should throw the first stone. Then He continued writing. In verses 9-11, John writes, "When they heard it, they began to go out one by one, beginning with the older ones, and He was left alone, and the woman, where she was, in the center of the court. Straightening up, Jesus said to her, 'Woman, where are they? Did no one condemn you?' She said, 'No one, Lord.' And Jesus said, 'I do not condemn you, either. Go. From now on sin no more.'" The people had brought her before Jesus for two reasons: They wanted to lure Jesus into saying something they could use against Him, and they had caught her in sin and wanted to see her condemned for it. They achieved neither of these objectives. Instead of condemnation, Jesus extended compassion and love. The only condemnation that occurred was when Jesus asked a question that required those who brought her to examine themselves and admit their own sin. Remember, we should expect the world to sin. Our job is to love them out of their sin and point them to Jesus. This is precisely what Jesus did when He did not condemn the woman, instead urging her to respond to His love and compassion by leaving her "life of sin." It is our responsibility to love the sinner, share the gospel of Jesus Christ, and urge them to respond by leaving their life of sin and turning to God.

How do we find these people? Does God bring them to us? Sometimes, God brings a lost soul to us, but if we are to follow Jesus' example, we can't just wait for people to come to us. We need to go in search of them. Jesus actively went looking for the lost. In Luke 19, we see the story of Zacchaeus. We all know the song about Zacchaeus. He wanted to see Jesus as He walked by, but he was too short to see over the crowd. He ran ahead and climbed up into a sycamore tree to see Him. Jesus stopped at the tree and told Zacchaeus to come down because He was going to stay at his house. Zacchaeus got down immediately, and almost immediately, people started complaining, saying Jesus had gone to be the "guest of a sinner." Zacchaeus stood up, and out of love and devotion to the Lord, vowed to give half his possessions to the poor and repay anyone he had cheated, four times the amount. In Luke 19:9-10, Jesus responded to him by saying, "Today salvation has come to this house, because he, too, is a son of Abraham. For the Son of Man has come to seek and to save that which was lost." Jesus knew the condition of Zacchaeus's soul and sought him out. He went from town to town, seeking those who were lost. The Pharisees and teachers of the law complained because Jesus ate with tax collectors and sinners. Jesus responded He came to call the sinners to repentance.

Jesus came because people were lost; they had no hope of eternal life. He came to find them and show them the way home to God. One of my favorite lost souls whom Jesus sought was a murderer and His choice to become His apostle to the Gentiles. Paul did not go looking for Jesus — Jesus came looking for him with a loud voice and a bright light. Paul, perhaps more than anyone else, understood the urgency of reaching the lost for Christ. He devoted his entire life, following his encounter with Jesus, to spreading the good news about Jesus Christ, at the risk of his own life. Paul writes in 1 Corinthians 9:19-23, For though I am free from all men, I have made myself a slave to all, so that I may win more. To the Jews I became as a Jew, so that

I might win Jews; to those who are under the Law, as under the Law though not being myself under the Law, so that I might win those who are under the Law; to those who are without law, as without law, though not being without the law of God but under the law of Christ, so that I might win those who are without law. To the weak I became weak, that I might win the weak; I have become all things to all men, so that I may by all means save some. I do all things for the sake of the gospel, so that I may become a fellow partaker of it.

Do you hear Paul's heart in the above passage? He says he made himself a slave to everyone, to win as many as possible. How do you get a heart like this for the lost? How do you see people the way Paul saw them? You get it the same way Paul did — by remembering what it was like to be lost. Paul remembered what it was like to live without Jesus — to be going in the wrong direction and deceived into thinking he was going the right way. Remembering how lost you were, how much you needed Jesus, and the joy of knowing Him, will renew your passion for the lost and inspire you to seek them out. Go on. What are you waiting for? Be bold. You have good news to share.

Bold Points to Ponder

- Read Luke 15:8-10. Share a time when you lost something dear to you and found it. What did you feel when you noticed it was missing; when you were looking for it; and when you found it?

- Have you ever been lost? Describe the feelings you had while lost and when you found your way.

- Read Acts 9:1-19; 22:1-16; 26:1-20.

    ◆ What was your first meeting like with Jesus when He found you?

    ◆ How did meeting Jesus change your life? The lives of those around you?

- Read 2 Peter 3:9 and Ezekiel 34:15-16. What do they tell you about God and His attitude toward humanity? What do they tell you about God's attitude toward you individually?

    ◆ What does knowing these things do for you, especially when you feel lost and distant from God?

- Read 1 Timothy 2:3-4 and Luke 19:10. Who are the lost? How does God see the lost? How did Jesus see them and treat them?

- Do you find it easier to focus on the sin in the world or the individual sinner?

    ◆ Read 2 Corinthians 7:8-10 and Matthew 5:14. What is the difference between godly sorrow and worldly sorrow?

- Do you agree that the politically correct term "unchurched" tends to remove the urgency and severity of the condition of the lost? Read Matthew 9:37-38 and Matthew 28:16-19. How do these verses apply to you and your Christian walk concerning the lost?

- Read Acts 17:24-26 and Ephesians 2:10. Think about where God has placed you. What is your individual mission field based on where God has put you?

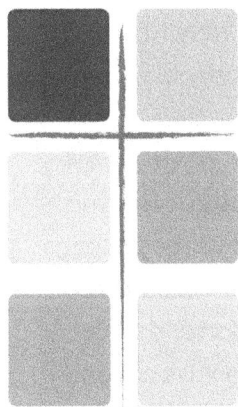

6

Discover Him

My family and I were enjoying a beautiful summer day at the amusement park, a place where happiness shines on children's faces. As I walked down a path, I heard wailing. Rounding a curve, I saw a little girl standing alone in the passing crowd, tears streaming down her face. I asked what was wrong. "Mommy!" was all she said. I took her little hand and assured her I would help find her mommy. After a few minutes, I spotted a woman frantically looking around and knew she must be searching for this sweet little girl. I stepped toward her, and when the little girl saw her, she let go of my hand and ran to her. The mother, overwhelmed with relief, wept tears of joy as they hugged one another. The lost one was found, and it was a time of rejoicing.

That's the way God feels when one of His lost ones is found. That's the way He felt about Paul. He was lost, but didn't know it.

Paul believed he was doing the work of God. He gave his approval of Stephen's stoning for his belief in Jesus (Acts 7:57-8:1). He traveled from town to town, rounding up men and women who followed Jesus, imprisoning them, and sentencing them to death because they believed Jesus was the Messiah and were followed His teachings. Paul was truly lost and writes in 1 Timothy 1:15, "It is a trustworthy statement, deserving full acceptance, that Christ Jesus came into the world to save sinners, among whom I am foremost of all." As lost as Paul was, Jesus sought him out, called him, and saved him. Then He used this former murderer to take the gospel of salvation and grace to the Gentiles and all who would listen (Acts 9:1-16). Never think that you can't be used by God or that you are too much of a sinner. Paul shows us that God can use anyone in the most extraordinary ways — if they are willing.

Washed Away

Like Paul, we were all lost at one time and have our own story to of how Jesus found and saved us. I identify with Paul's story. Like many others, I believed I was saved because I had "prayed Christ into my heart," read my Bible, lived a good life, shared Jesus, and helped others accept Christ. I truly thought I was doing what God wanted and that I was teaching the truth. Then I came home for summer break and learned about someone in my community who had left the church of her youth and was living for Jesus. We weren't close, but I needed a church to go to, so I called her. She told me about a church she was attending where they took the Bible seriously and earnestly lived by it. She invited me to go, so I did.

It was a Wednesday night meeting, and afterward, people my age were going out for ice cream. I went along, not knowing my life was about to be turned upside down. I overheard someone say he wanted to be baptized and become a Christian. *What is he talking about?* I thought. *You don't have to be baptized to be a Christian. You can do that after you're a Christian.* Being outnumbered, I said nothing but couldn't get it out of my head all night. The next day, I went downtown to the public library and, using their concordance along with my Bible, I looked up every scripture I could find on baptism. I also checked a Greek dictionary to see what the word meant. I was surprised to find that being baptized meant to be immersed or submerged. When I finished, I closed my Bible and thought, *I'm not a Christian! I need to be baptized for my sins to be forgiven and to receive the Holy Spirit.* It was quite a revelation and a shock. Realizing I was still in sin and without the Holy Spirit took the wind out of me. I wondered why no one had ever told me what baptism was really about. All I knew for sure was that it was urgent to get this right. I took the bus home and decided the next time I went to church I would talk with someone about getting baptized.

Learning I was lost was terrible. Every night I had nightmares about dying before I could get baptized. I'd wake up in a cold sweat, praying that God wouldn't take me before my sins were washed away. Thankfully, He answered that prayer, and in just a few days, I was baptized. An overwhelming sense of relief and peace filled me when I came up out of the water in the minister's pool. I knew then that I belonged to Christ, and my life has never been the same.

Eternal Importance

I pray that you can see how vitally important it is that we share the entire gospel with people. I had been going along believing my sins had been forgiven only to find out later I lacked something of great importance, much like the disciples in Ephesus who only knew the baptism of John for repentance. They had never been baptized into Christ and received the Holy Spirit. Paul had to explain the way of salvation more clearly to them so they could truly give their lives to Christ in baptism and receive forgiveness of sins and the Holy Spirit (Acts 19:1-7). Sharing the full gospel of Christ and how to become a Christian is the most important mission God has given us. We do not want to have someone ask us later, "Why didn't you tell me?"

We all have our own story to tell, because we all started in the same place — lost. Remembering where we came from and what it felt like to be lost — the fear, anxiety, and urgency to become one with Christ — helps us have a heart for the lost. Our eyes need to be open to their plight. Each non-Christian we meet is standing on the edge of a cliff, and we may be the one to pull them back. I once read something in a book that has really shaped how I see a non-believer. A man named Dr. Lester Sumrall claimed to have had a vision in which he saw masses of people walking along a very wide highway:

> "God lifted me up until I was looking down upon that uncountable multitude of humankind. He took me far down the highway until I saw the end of the road. It ended abruptly at a precipice towering above a bottomless inferno. When the tremendous unending procession of people came to the end of the highway, I could see them falling off into eternity. As they neared the pit and saw the fate that awaited them, I could see their desperate but vain struggle to push back against the unrelenting pressure of those to the rear. The great surging river of humanity swept them ever forward. God opened my ears to hear the screams of damned souls sinking into hell... I could see their faces distorted with terror. Their hands flailed wildly, clawing at the air."[1]

---

1.   Sumrall, L., and J.S. Conn. Sumrall Publishing, *Run with the Vision*, 2003.

I don't know if his vision was from God or not, but regardless, it is a vivid picture for us of the overwhelming number of people on the broad road leading to destruction and what awaits them. This description has helped me to see the lost differently. It has helped me to remember the reality of what they face. How can we refuse to share Jesus with people so in need? How can we turn away?

Paul makes it clear that God has a job for us to do. In 2 Corinthians 5:16-20, Paul puts that job into focus for us. As Christians, we are to reach out to the lost and "implore/beg" them to be reconciled with God. We are not to look at people from a worldly view, but a spiritual one. Every person we meet can either live in eternal torment or eternal peace and happiness. God says He is making His appeal to the lost through His children — us. God uses us to make a difference in their eternity.

Offering of Hope

As Christian women, we are to hold out the message of reconciliation to God through Jesus Christ. So many people need to hear that God loves them. They need to hear that no matter how they have lived, or are living now, God will forgive them. We have to let them know that there is hope found in Jesus Christ — a hope that speaks of grace, mercy, forgiveness, love, and eternal life. So many are without hope of these things, and we have it to offer to them. In Ephesians 2:10, Paul writes, "For we are God's handiwork, created in Christ Jesus to do good works, which God prepared in advance for us to do" (NIV). One of the good works He has prepared for us to do is to reach out to the lost with the gospel of Jesus Christ and the promise of eternal life. We have what they need to get off that highway to hell and hopelessness and on to the narrow road that leads to hope and heaven. God puts lost people in our path. We must open our eyes to see them and have a heart of compassion to love them, like Jesus does.

One incident that illustrates Jesus' love and compassion for each person individually is found in Luke 8:40-48. Jesus has returned to Galilee and is greeted by a crowd. Jairus, a synagogue official falls at Jesus' feet and implores Him to heal his 12-year-old daughter who is dying. While on His way, a woman somehow manages to make it through the crowd to touch the hem of Jesus' garment. She had been suffering for 12 years with a bleeding disorder that not only left her poor and weak, but also unclean according to Jewish law. Jesus knew someone had touched Him and asked who did. It's amazing that in the midst of a crowd following Him and pushing around Him, He still noticed this one woman. She eventually came forward and told why she had done so. Jesus' response to her was "Daughter, your faith has made you well; go in peace." He then continued on to raise Jairus' daughter from the dead, as she had died while He was on His way. Take note that Jesus noticed this one woman among the multitude and took the time to meet her need. Jesus is the Savior of the world, but He is that Savior by being the Savior of the individual.

Responsible Privilege

The world is saved one person at a time. God uses each of us, His people who have experienced salvation through Jesus Christ, to reach those in our sphere of influence. We must open our eyes to the lost around us. Sharing Jesus with the lost is a tremendous responsibility, but it is also a privilege. When we share Him and His love with a person and see the joy with which they receive it, our hearts fill with joy as well. For me, when someone decides to follow Jesus, it brings back everything I felt when I answered His call to follow Him and gave my life to Him. It is a joy to be reminded of that, because we lose the wonder of it after being a Christian for a while. Having my wonder and excitement at being a Christian revived with each new sister in Christ keeps me from taking it for granted.

As wonderful as that is, in my humanity, all too often, my fears and insecurities get the best of me and prevent me from sharing my faith. We all want to be liked. We all want to be included and fit in with people. That desire to be liked and fit in can cause us to be afraid to share Jesus, to stand up for Christian values, morals, and purity. We fear offending someone. We are afraid of so many things — being made fun of, rejected, getting into an argument, looking different. However, we can't let this stop us. James 4:17 says, "If anyone, then, knows the good they ought to do and doesn't do it, it is sin for them" (NIV). Certainly, sharing our faith in Jesus with the lost is "good," and we must do it. That is our primary mission in life — to share Christ with people and bring as many as possible to a saving faith in Him. There is another common fear that often stops us from sharing Christ — the one that says you just don't know enough. We do not have to be scholars to do this. Remember, it all started with a group of uneducated fishermen. All we have to know is who Jesus is, what He did for us, and what our response should be.

Maybe you're already doing a great job at reaching out to the lost, but I'm fearful that many are not. In Luke 15:4-7, Jesus told this parable: "What man among you, if he has a hundred sheep and has lost one of them, does not leave the ninety-nine in the open pasture and go after the one which is lost until he finds it? When he has found it, he lays it on his shoulders, rejoicing. And when he comes home, he calls together his friends and his neighbors, saying to them, 'Rejoice with me, for I have found my sheep which was lost!' I tell you that in the same way, there will be more joy in heaven over one sinner who repents than over ninety-nine righteous persons who need no repentance."

We spend a lot of our time with the "ninety-nine," the righteous, the people in God's church. How much time do we spend looking for the lost sheep, the one who will cause such rejoicing in heaven — and in our own hearts — when they are found? It is much easier to hang out with the "ninety-nine" than to go out looking for the one. But that is exactly what God calls us to do.

We have a lot of fellowship activities in our churches. That means we spend a lot of time together, which is a great thing. Consider this: How much time do we spend looking for the lost sheep, the one who will cause such rejoicing in heaven when found? Though we need to spend time with the family of God, we also must be out there looking for that lost sheep so we can bring them into the fold. It's good to be with the "ninety-nine," but there are people out there dying, waiting for us to find them. We have to get out of our comfort zones and get out there. We've got to open our eyes!

Ripe for the Harvest

We all know the story of Jesus talking with the Samaritan woman at the well. I want to focus for a minute on what happened *after* their conversation. Jesus has just finished speaking with the woman, revealing that He is the Messiah she has been expecting, when His disciples show up. They've been off buying food and are surprised to find Jesus talking with this woman. The woman runs off. She doesn't even take her water jar with her because she's in a hurry to tell people about Jesus. Let's look at John 4:29-35, starting with what the woman shares with the townspeople. "Come, see a man who told me all the things that I have done; this is not the Christ, is it?" They went out of the city, and were coming to Him. Meanwhile the disciples were urging Him, saying, "Rabbi, eat." But He said to them, "I have food to eat that you do not know about." So the disciples were saying to one another, "No one brought Him anything to eat, did he?" Jesus said to them, "My food is to do the will of Him who sent Me and to accomplish His work. "Do you not say, 'There are yet four months, and then comes the harvest'? Behold, I say to you, lift up your eyes and look on the fields, that they are white for harvest.'"

Don't you find it interesting that Jesus turned the conversation with His disciples around to the harvest? What was happening as He told them to open their eyes and look at the fields? The townspeople, those to whom the Samaritan woman had rushed off to tell about Jesus, were coming toward them. There was the harvest! There were the lost sheep, following the least-likely person to meet the shepherd. The fields are ripe for harvest! I'll prove it to you.

Did you know that according to the Barna Group, the most effective way to get people to visit a church is through a personal invitation by a friend? About 20 percent of those surveyed "expressed a strong interest," and nearly 50 percent were "willing to consider a church based on this factor." Unfortunately, this is in a downward trend. "Twenty years ago, two-thirds of churchless Americans (65%) were open to being invited to church by a friend." However, it is still the most effective way of reaching out to the churchless. The definition being used here for churchless is people who "have not attended a Christian church service, other than a special event such as a wedding or a funeral, at any time during the past six months." As of 2014, the Barna Group estimated there were 156 million unchurched, including children and teenagers, in the United States. Of course, that number has surely increased over the last 10 years. Now if you do the math, adding the 20 percent with a strong interest in accepting an invitation to church to the nearly 50 percent willing to consider accepting an invitation, that would be 118,560,000 people who might attend church if invited. So, what's happening? Why are all these people not attending church? Could it be we aren't inviting them? The Barna Group tells us that "nearly two-thirds of churched Christians (64%) say they're open to inviting someone to attend an in-person service." We're "open" to inviting people, but how many of follow through and do it? If we did, there would be more visitors regularly in our congregations.

The fields are ripe for harvest! We must open our eyes! Why can't we see it? Are we so focused on our own lives — work, kids, spouses, church activities, etc. — that we cannot see the lost souls crying out for help around us? We get lost in our busyness and do not stop long enough to look up and see what is around us. We must take our mission of sharing the gospel seriously and take advantage of every opportunity the Lord puts before us. Proverbs 10:5 says, "He who gathers in summer is a son who acts wisely, But he who sleeps in harvest is a son who acts shamefully." Are we awake, gathering the crops and planting new seeds, or are we sleeping through the harvest, thinking someone else more gifted at evangelism will do it? If we are sleeping, if we are not active in the harvest of the lost, Scripture says we are disgraceful children.

Why don't we share our faith more? Why do we shy away from inviting people to worship or church activities? Let's revisit our fears. Earlier, I said that we are afraid that others might think we're strange or different. Well, we are. We are afraid they will say no. We are afraid we won't be accepted. If we give into our fears, we are playing directly into the hands of Satan. He wants us paralyzed with fear so that God's kingdom will not advance. We cannot let this happen! People are hungry to hear about the love and grace of God — they just need someone, us, to tell them about it.

Let me close this chapter by sharing a recent experience that spoke to my heart. My husband's company was celebrating its 50th anniversary, and they threw a couple of parties for employees and their spouses. They sponsored a private "Taste of Syracuse" reception. The food was great, the conversation lively, and the music wonderful. All evening, various bands were playing in different areas of the reception. Just before dark, one group started to sing "Amazing Grace." The entire crowd of about 1,000 people stopped talking and listened. No other song that evening, before or after this one, had that effect. As they sang, I looked around in amazement. Everyone just stood there listening — the eating and talking had almost completely stopped. A song about the grace of God had the ability to quiet 1,000 people because it touched a place in their hearts that is starving for God's grace and hungry to hear about salvation through Jesus Christ. The harvest truly is plentiful. Let's be some of the much-needed workers to join the Lord in seeking the lost and rejoicing as each one is found.

Bold Points to Ponder

- How did God pursue you? What is your story about how God saved you?

- Read Romans 9:14,15 and Galatians 6:1, 2. What is your responsibility as a Christian regarding the lost people around you and what should be your demeanor when approaching them?

- Look again at Galatians 6:1, 2 and read Romans 15:1, 2. What warning and admonition did Paul give us?

- Have you shared the good news of Jesus with someone and had the privilege to watch her give her life to Christ? If so, describe how you felt?

- Read Luke 8:40-48. Jesus was always aware of the people around Him and their needs. What changes, if any, can you make so you can be like Jesus in this way?

- What, if anything, gets in the way of your going out in search of the lost and sharing the gospel with them?

- Read 1 Corinthians 1:20 -24; 2:1 – 5; Acts 4:13. What do you need to know to reach out to the lost and share the good news of Jesus?

- Look back at the statistics quoted from Barna Research Group. When is the last time you invited someone to church? What has prevented you from inviting people to church?

- Have you ever gone out from the "ninety-nine" and been rejected? How did that make you feel?

  - Read John 15:18-25. What do these verses tell you about the rejection you experience when sharing the gospel?

- Share a time when you witnessed God at work around you. What effect did it have on you?

7

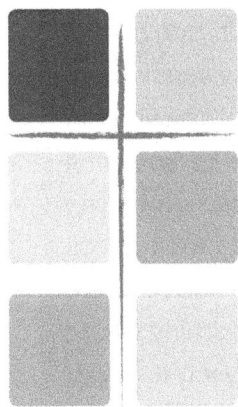

Embrace His Will

From a young age, I have loved books. One of many fond memories of my childhood was my father dropping my sisters and me off at the public library on Saturday mornings. Every few weeks, we would pile into the car, our arms laden with books to return. Once at the library, I would comb the shelves in the children's section, picking out my next stack of books to take home. After checking them out, I would return to the children's section, find a place on the floor amongst the bookshelves, and read until my father returned. Books were my constant companions. I would read before school, often losing track of time, which meant running to arrive before the late bell had rung. During lunch, I would again lose myself in a book, and after school, I would run up the stairs to my room and lie on my bed to read until dinnertime.

I continue to have a passion for books and reading, and many of my friends are passionate about other things: shopping, exercise, nutrition, hobbies, or even food. People will talk your ears off about the latest miracle-working supplement. They talk with such passion and enthusiasm about it, convincing you to try it. It makes me sad that so many of us speak more passionately about something as inconsequential as a vitamin supplement but not about Jesus. Shouldn't we be speaking about Jesus, our Lord and Savior, with at least the same intensity we use when talking about the new unbelievable weight loss injection? Once, I found myself in a conversation about where the best soft ice cream is in my area. There was nothing wrong with that conversation, but it made me ask myself if I even knew the last time I had as enthusiastic a conversation about Jesus. All ice cream does is add inches to my waistline. Jesus? He allowed Himself to be whipped to the point of death and then willingly finished that death for me on the cross. So, which one deserves my time and devotion? Being passionate about our hobbies, families, or anything else is perfectly fine, but we should be careful to keep some perspective.

Let's think about the church for a minute. There is an often-quoted statistic you've probably heard. "In a church, 80 percent of the work is done by 20 percent of the people." Another common term is "pew warmer." It usually means people who come on Sunday, but other than that one hour per week, they are not involved in the life of the church. Why is it that only 20 percent of the people do the work? Why do our churches have so many pew warmers? There are many reasons, but it really boils down to a lack of passion. Our churches are doing so many wonderful things — adult and children's Bible classes, youth groups and activities, ice cream socials, fellowship meals, prison ministries, women's Bible studies, food pantries, clothing giveaways, and the list could go on. Even so, we have many pew warmers.

Though we all are passionate about something, fervor seems to be lacking in the church today. What does it even mean to be passionate? According to Merriam-Webster, *passion* is "an ardent affection; a strong liking or desire for or devotion to some activity, object, or concept." This is the definition of which we are most aware. This is where that passion for the best soft ice cream comes in. What, though, is passion for a Christian? As always, Jesus will be our example.

Conscious of Purpose

If we want to know where our passion should lie, then we need to understand what Jesus was passionate about. Let's turn our attention to John 4 and Jesus' encounter with the Samaritan woman. As the woman leaves to tell the people in her village about Jesus, the disciples return with the food they purchased. John 4:31-34 says, "Meanwhile his disciples urged him, 'Rabbi, eat something.' But he said to them, 'I have food to eat that you know nothing about.' Then his disciples said to each other, 'Could someone have brought him food?' 'My food,' said Jesus, 'is to do the will of him who sent me and to finish his work'" (NIV).

The most basic human needs are food, water, and shelter. Many people, for instance, are obsessed with food. We even have a name for them — foodies — and TV networks devoted to all things food. Jesus' idea of food differs from the disciples' or ours. They were thinking physical, and once again, Jesus brought them to the spiritual. His food, His most basic need, His passion "is to do the will of Him who sent" Him and to "finish His work." Jesus had passion, but it wasn't for food or anything else this world could give Him. His passion was doing His Father's will. This was His number one priority, and it always had been.

We can see Jesus putting His Father's will first in the account of Jesus at the temple at the age of 12. Jesus had gone to Jerusalem with His family for the Passover feast. After the Passover, his parents and relatives left. They had been traveling for about a day before realizing Jesus wasn't with them. They hurried back to Jerusalem to look for Him. It took another three days, but they found Him, sitting in the temple with the teachers, listening and asking questions. His parents questioned Him about why He had stayed behind without their knowledge. He responded, "Why is it that you were looking for Me? Did you not know that I had to be in My Father's house?" (Luke 2:49). In the New King James Version, it reads, "Did you not know that I must be about my Father's business?"

Jesus said He "had to be" in His Father's house; He must be about His Father's business. The words *had to be* and *must* show that this was a real desire on His part. This was at the age of 12. Jesus's words to His disciples about His food being to do His Father's will, came at about age 30. His priorities had not changed. He was clear — doing His Father's will was His number one priority. In John 6:38, Jesus says it again, "For I have come down from heaven, not to do My own will, but the will of Him who sent Me." Throughout Jesus' life here on earth, the overriding purpose of His life, what fed Him, fed His soul, was to do the will of His Father. Throughout the Scriptures, we can see that what drove Christ was doing God's will. He was conscious of His purpose, and He put obedience to His Father above all else.

In Luke 4, we again witness Jesus' focus on obedience to God. He is spending the night in Simon's home and is asked to help Simon's mother-in-law because she is sick with a high fever. Jesus heals her. As the sun sets, a crowd shows up at Simon's house. News of Jesus' being there had caused the people to bring the sick to Him for healing. Verse 40 says, "and laying His hands on each one of them, He was healing them." Not only did He heal illnesses, but He also freed people from various demons. Let's pick up in verse 42-44: It is the morning after all the healings, and we read, "When day came, Jesus left and went to a secluded place; and the crowds were searching for Him, and came to Him and tried to keep Him from going away from them. But He said to them, 'I must preach the kingdom of God to the other cities also, for I was sent for this purpose.' So He kept on preaching in the synagogues of Judea." Though Jesus loved the people and wanted to help them, He knew He had to go. It was God's will for Him to go to the other towns and preach the good news of the kingdom of God. He could have stayed and done some good, but He was obedient to the will of God and went to preach in other towns.

Decision Time

We are often faced with decisions like this. We have the option of spending our time on something that is good, and maybe even something we desire to do, but God has something else in mind for us. When I was in college, I went home almost every weekend. By bus, my travel time was over four hours, but it was worth it. I would get to see my family, have a home-cooked meal, and attend church. Those Sunday night bus rides back to school, however, seemed to take a lot longer than the rides home. Typically, I used the time to read the Bible and do some homework. I looked forward to that uninterrupted time of reading God's Word. One Sunday night, I was reading my Bible when we stopped to pick up someone. I was deep into my reading, so I didn't even look up as she got on the bus. She stopped at my row, though, and asked if she could sit next to me. When I looked up, I was surprised to see a nun standing there waiting for my answer. I told her she was welcome and made room for her.

I hoped she wasn't a talkative person, because I wanted to keep reading the Bible. After a couple of minutes, she interrupted my reading with a question: "Why are you reading the Bible?" I thought it an odd question, coming from a nun, but I replied, "Because I want to know God better, understand His plan, and learn how He would like me to live." She asked me if I was Catholic. I told her I had been raised Catholic, but I was no longer a Catholic. "I'm just a Christian. I read the Bible and do my best to live by it." She asked me why I left the church, and I responded, "There are too many teachings of the Catholic church that are either not found in the Bible or are against what the Bible teaches." She seemed surprised and asked if I would show her some of what I was talking about. We talked about the baptism of babies, and I told her there is not one instance of a baby being baptized in the Bible. I could see the look of shock on her face.

She asked me to give her some other examples, and I opened my Bible to Mark 7:5-13, specifically verses 6-9. "He replied, 'Isaiah was right when he prophesied about you hypocrites; as it is written: 'These people honor me with their lips, but their hearts are far from me. They worship me in vain; their teachings are merely human rules.' You have let go of the commands of God and are holding on to human traditions.' And he continued, 'You have a fine way of setting aside the commands of God in order to observe your own traditions!'" (NIV). I told her that a priest once told me that if it came down to following the Bible or the traditions of the church, he assured me he would follow the tradition. I asked her if that was true, and she acknowledged that it was. I could, however, see the doubt creeping into her eyes. I then recounted to her a disagreement I had had with my parents. They were angry that I would not call a priest "Father" or another priest "Monsignor." I had asked them what Monsignor meant only to find out it meant "My Lord." I explained to the nun that I just could not do it. She asked why, so I turned to Matthew 23:8-9 and read, "But do not be called Rabbi; for One is your Teacher, and you are all brothers. Do not call anyone on earth your father; for One is your Father, He who is in heaven." I said to her, "That is why I can't call a priest 'Father.' I would be going against what Jesus taught." We spoke of a few more things and then arrived at her bus stop.

She got up to go, walked a few steps, and turned around. Looking me in the eyes, she said, "You have given me a lot to think about. Thank you." Then, with a look of sadness, yet a bit of a sparkle in her eye, she said, "I may have to make a major change." She got off the bus, and I sat praying, thanking God that He stopped me from doing something good — reading my Bible — and opened my eyes to the opportunity He put in my path. I don't know if she ever made the change she referenced, but I am so glad that I spoke with her instead of reading my Bible. Reading my Bible was good, but sharing God's Word with someone who needed to hear it was so much better. Jesus said in Luke 4:43, "I must preach the kingdom of God to the other cities also, for I was sent for this purpose." Healing people was good, but preaching the good news was God's will for Jesus. Jesus chose what was best.

Jesus knew what God's will was for His life on earth and what His purpose was, and He told us in His own words. Jesus did a lot of good while on the earth, but first and foremost, He knew what was best and was laser focused on putting God's will first at all times. He was passionately obedient to His Father.

In 1846, Soren Kierkegaard wrote *Purity of Heart Is to Will One Thing*. The "one thing" about which he was speaking was "will the good." Though I disagree with Kierkegaard on many things and can't quite understand what he was saying about other things,

I agree that purity of heart is to will one thing. Kierkegaard calls it "the good" — I say purity of heart is to desire God's will above all else. Jesus put God's will above everything else, even to the point of sacrificing His own life on the cross — it was the reason He was here.

Will First

The first disciples learned from Jesus what it meant to put God's will first. They were passionate about the Lord and about spreading the good news of Jesus and the salvation He freely extends to all. They had an urgency to preach this good news, just as Jesus did.

Serving the Lord and spreading the gospel was the purpose of their lives. They left families, friends, jobs, and well, everything to serve Jesus Christ. They followed Him while He lived and went to their deaths for Him after He ascended into heaven. I want to live like that, don't you? Fulfilling God's will must be the greatest priority of our lives. If it is, we will possess that same urgency and commitment. We won't let fear stop us from taking a stand. Each day, when we wake up, we will be determined to make a difference for the Lord and be filled with excitement at what the day may bring. Each day, God places opportunities in our paths. We must open our eyes to see them and then do our best to fulfill the assignment, to make a difference for the kingdom.

That is how it should be for us as individuals, but what about the church, our congregations? Think about your own congregation. Do you see passion, commitment, involvement? Jesus said in Revelation 3:15-16, "I know your deeds, that you are neither cold nor hot; I wish that you were cold or hot. So because you are lukewarm, and neither hot nor cold, I will spit you out of My mouth." What are we? What are our congregations? Are we hot? Are we cold? I fear we are becoming lukewarm, if we haven't already.

For clarification, I do not wish to imply that every individual in the church is lukewarm. Many are passionate about Jesus and the gospel, who willingly and eagerly devote their days to serving Him and spreading the gospel. In fact, your reading this is indicative that you are either "hot" or you desire to rekindle that fire within yourself. You are not lukewarm. Still, I think this is something we must all think about.

Writing this book has me looking back to the time, all those years ago, that I became a Christian. It was an exciting time. Spiritual conversations were the norm. When our young adult group got together for anything, — pizza, a movie, ice cream, or just "hanging out" — the conversations were almost always about Jesus, the Bible, what we were learning, and how we were changing. We would talk late into the night and go home feeling energized and spiritually filled. We were passionate about Jesus and spiritual things — we were "hot." Colossians 4:6 truly describes this time of my life. It says, "Let your speech always be with grace, as though seasoned with salt, so that you will know how you should respond to each person." I think one of the ways we learn how to answer everyone is by talking with one another about what God is teaching us through the Scriptures, discussing the Bible, and learning from one another. These kinds of conversations feed our passion for the Lord and help us grow and mature. Being in the Bible, learning, and sharing what God is teaching us is something we want; but it is more than that — it is something we need.

Unfortunately, many in the church have things backwards. Too many of us do everything we see as necessary in life, or important in life, and then use our leftover time to spend with God, His people, and serving Him. This is definitely backwards.

Spending time with God, serving Christ, and living for Christ should be our first priority. Everything else should get "fit in." Instead, we "fit in" our Bible reading. We "fit in" our prayer times. We "fit in" time to help fellow Christians. We "fit in" spending time with an unbeliever who really needs to see Christ in us. And the worst thing? We "fit in" sharing the message of Jesus and His salvation. When I look back on the young adult years of my life, I remember it being the other way around. I remember the struggle was how to fit in everything else around Jesus. He, the church, and the lost were my focus. I could no more stop talking about my faith than I could stop breathing. Somewhere along the line, this changed for many of us, and it became time to get back to what we once knew. I am so grateful that Jesus didn't just "fit in" ministering to those around Him; I am so grateful that obeying the will of His Father was paramount to Him. If Jesus had gone to watch the local theater production instead of healing both body and soul, where would we be today?

Our Example

Remember, Jesus is our example. When John the Baptist was beheaded, and Jesus wanted to get away to be with the Father to mourn the loss of this great servant of God, a crowd followed Him. He could have said, "Leave Me alone. I need time to be alone and grieve." Instead, He had compassion for them and put their needs first. He had just lost someone He dearly loved, but He put the needs of the crowd above His own. Years ago, a close friend of mine suffered a tremendous loss. His fiancé was to meet him at another friend's rehearsal dinner. She never came. Later that night, the police found her car upside down in a frozen creek. The next day, divers found her frozen under the ice, her hands wrapped around a cross she wore. The diver who found her later said he had never seen anything like it. With tears streaming down his face, he said she looked like an angel, and he was sure she'd been praying because her face was a vision of peace. At the visitation, I watched in amazement as my friend ministered to and comforted one person after another. He was in the midst of unbelievable grief, but he put that aside to take care of the needs of others. Like Jesus, he put the needs of the crowd above his own. Letting the light of Jesus Christ shine through our lives, serving God by serving others, and doing God's will should dictate the way we live, no matter what the circumstances.

Jesus remains our example for every situation in life. His example of living selflessly and meeting the needs of others shows us how we are to live. How are you doing in this area? Think about this simple example. You're watching a TV show that you are enjoying when your phone rings. You answer it, but you quickly brush off the person on the other end, promising to call them back. Now think about what your actions conveyed. In essence, you were saying that TV show(or whatever else you were doing) was more important than spending a little time with someone on the phone — a person who may have sincerely needed to talk, who needed encouragement, but you wouldn't know because you didn't take the time to listen. Hebrews 10:24 advises, "… and let us consider how to stimulate one another to love and good deeds." **We must consider. We must think** about what we say and do and examine ourselves to make sure we are putting God's will first and above our own. That was the message of Jesus' life — God first — and He lived it every day.

As Christians, our food, what sustains us, is the same as Jesus' food. If we live on the same food Jesus did, we will experience the spiritual fire in our hearts and lives. Do you want to experience true joy in your life? Make Christ's passion, your passion. Do God's will, and accomplish the work He has prepared for you, and you'll be filled to overflowing with joy, excitement, and God's peace. Take your eyes off yourself and your desires and put your focus back on God. Doing God's will is what you were made for, and it is the only way you will ever truly be fulfilled.

Bold Points to Ponder

- What are some things you are passionate about? How does talking about your passion with someone else make you feel?

- Describe what you think a "pew warmer" looks like?

- Read John 4:34; 9:4; and 17:4. Jesus' passion was to do the will of His Father. He was passionate about being obedient to His Father and doing His work. Describe what someone who shares the same passion as Christ would look like today?

- Have you ever been involved in doing something good, but felt God calling you to move on to something else? If so, what did you feel at the time and what did you do?

- Read these verses and write down what each says about Jesus' purpose on earth. Matthew 5:17; Matthew 20:28; Luke 19:10; John 3:17; John 10:10; John 18:37

- Read Acts 4:12-22 and Acts 5:17-29.

  - Discuss a time you found yourself in a position requiring you to be bold and go against the "crowd" because of your faith.

- Read Psalm 19:14 and Colossians 3:16–17. Think about the last time you were with a group of Christians and the conversations you had.

  - Write down some ways you can begin a spiritual conversation with another Christian.

  - Conversely, write down some ways you can begin a spiritual conversation with a non-Christian.

- Jesus' commitment to His mission, to sharing God and salvation with everyone, was paramount throughout His life.

  - How do you sacrifice what you want to do or had planned to do to meet the needs of others?

- Read Matthew 6:25-34, with special attention to verses 33 and 34.

  - What changes can you make to better fulfill this command and your purpose as a follower of Christ?

8

Valuable Life

My aunt is amazing. She is only a few years older than I am, so she is more like a sister. We grew up together, got into trouble together, and learned from each other. Once, when I was in middle school, my sisters decided to prank me. Thankfully, my aunt found out about it and told me what they had done, saving me from a lot of embarrassment. To this day, I am grateful she cared more about protecting me than whatever fallout she would experience with my sisters.

My aunt's life hasn't always been easy, but she rises above everything that might hold her back. When she was in her mid-to-late 20s and newly divorced, she knew she had to make a change. She went back to school and received her occupational therapy degree and license. After working for the State of New York for a year, she signed up as a traveling occupational therapist.

She traveled the country, staying in each destination for three months before moving on to the next, eventually settling in California. Over the years, being smart with her money afforded her many opportunities. She has traveled all over the world, sometimes with friends, sometimes by herself. She is fearless and has let nothing stop her— not divorce, her sisters' deaths, her mother's death, not cancer, or surgeries. She has grabbed onto life and lives it to the fullest. Now retired, she recently became a Christian and still travels, enjoys her friends, and all that life has to offer. As a Christian, she is bringing that same zest for life to how she lives out her Christianity. I admire her ability to live, holding nothing back.

All In for Christ

My desire, as a Christian, is to live like that. I want the energy, excitement, and fulfillment that comes from being "all in" for Jesus. Jesus said in John 10:10, "The thief comes only to steal and kill and destroy; I came that they may have life, and have it abundantly." Satan is the thief. His goal is to steal our faith and confidence in God, to kill us spiritually and destroy any hope we have of eternal life. Jesus offers the opposite. His desire is for us to experience a full, abundant life here and eternal life with Him when our work here is finished. We have only one life to live on this earth; it should be something we live to the fullest.

In writing this, I am reminded of the two disciples traveling the road on the way to Emmaus shortly after Jesus' crucifixion. As they walked, talking about all that had happened in Jerusalem and the death of Jesus, a man began walking with them. Not realizing it was Jesus, they informed Him of all the terrible things that had happened, including the disappearance of Jesus' body and the women's insistence that an angel said He was alive. Jesus gently explained to them that the Messiah had to suffer and then explained to them everything the Scriptures said about Himself. Eventually, they stopped to eat. The men still didn't recognize Him, but when Jesus blessed the bread, broke it, and gave it to them, they suddenly realized who He was. Luke 24:32 says, "They said to one another, 'Were not our hearts burning within us while He was speaking to us on the road, while He was explaining the Scriptures to us?'" I want my heart to burn with the knowledge of who Jesus is and the desire to be close to Him and live for Him. With Jesus, our lives can be filled to overflowing. Because of Him, our lives can be extraordinary.

What makes a life extraordinary? For many, it means being successful in business, amassing a fortune, being able to do whatever they want, or living a life that fulfills all their desires. For the Christian, the extraordinary life is completely different. The people we see as being extraordinary are people who give of themselves for others. They sacrifice their time, money, energy, even their lives in service to others, because by serving them, they serve God. A good example of this is a woman named Corrie ten Boom. She and her family hid Jewish families from the Nazis, were arrested, and sent to a concentration camp. While there, her faith sustained her as she took care of her sister and the other women around her. She encouraged them with her love for Christ and led worship services using a Bible they were able to sneak in. Her faith in Jesus and how she practiced that faith made her life extraordinary. She was totally surrendered to God and His will, regardless of her circumstances.

You might think you'll never have anything but an ordinary life. That isn't true. Jesus showed us what it means to lead an extraordinary life as a Christian. He made the most of the time He had, not for His own enjoyment, but for God. Doing the will of God and finishing His work was always on His mind and guided everything He did.

There is a couple from my congregation who come closer to living as Jesus did than anyone I've ever met. They work tirelessly for the Lord as a team, even while dealing with trials and health problems of their own. They have taken complete strangers into their home, studied the Scriptures with individuals and groups, mentored many in the church, visited those in the hospital, studied with those in prison, given away their possessions to those in need, fed the hungry, and the husband shepherded the flock here for almost 50 years. They are so mindful of being good stewards of everything with which God has blessed them that they buy their clothes at the thrift store, so they will have more to share. They are two of the dearest people in my life and have taught me so much about following Jesus and surrendering all to Him. They have been a living, breathing example to me of what it means to lead an extraordinary life in Christ. Their only goal is to follow Jesus and offer themselves up to Him in worship.

The secret to living an extraordinary life for God is simple:

* Make the most of the time you have here for God. Know your purpose is to do His will and let that be the guiding principle you live by.

* Serve God by serving others.

Live an Extraordinary Life

Matthew 20:26-28 teaches, "whoever wishes to become great among you shall be your servant, and whoever wishes to be first among you shall be your slave; just as the Son of Man did not come to be served, but to serve, and to give His life a ransom for many." Living the extraordinary life may be simple, but it is never easy. Living the way God has called each of us to live is difficult. We live in a world obsessed with entertainment, pleasure, individual rights, and a "me-first" attitude. These things are opposite of how Jesus lived and how God has called us to live. Living the abundant life in Christ is a constant battle. Too often, we walk through life on autopilot. Worldly attitudes slowly creep into our lives, whether we want them or not, because our focus keeps shifting away from our purpose.

Satan is adept at distracting us. He knows just what will make us take our eyes off Jesus. Years ago, I saw the animated movie, *Up*. One of the most popular characters of the movie is a dog named Dug, who is unusual because he can speak. He joins the heroes of the movie, guiding them and helping them to overcome the villain. He does a great job until someone says the word *squirrel*. As soon as Dug hears that word, his head snaps around in search of a squirrel. It doesn't matter what he is doing at the time, his entire focus becomes the squirrel. We aren't all that different from Dug. Satan knows our weaknesses, and whenever we become too useful for Christ, too focused on our mission, he yells *squirrel*, and our heads snap away from what we should be doing to something else.

It would be great if we could blame all our distractions and failures on Satan Unfortunately, we excel at distracting ourselves without his help. Sometimes, we enjoy this world too much, living as if this is all there is, putting our own desires, enjoyment, and feelings first. God warns us about getting caught up in the things of the world in 1 John 2:15-17. "Do not love the world nor the things in the world. If anyone loves the world, the love of the Father is not in him. For all that is in the world, the lust of the flesh and the lust of the eyes and the boastful pride of life, is not from the Father, but is from the world. The world is passing away, and also its lusts; but the one who does the will of God lives forever." Our love for the things of this world is not intentional. It creeps up and into our lives, taking our eyes off our purpose — doing the will of God. These verses remind us and serve as a warning to us that everything in the world will pass away. It reminds us that if we do God's will, if we remain faithful to Him, we will live forever. There is nothing in this world worth giving up our eternity. We must not let ourselves get so caught up in enjoying life here that we don't keep in mind the far better life that is yet to come. Like Jesus, we need to understand how temporary this physical life is and keep our eyes focused on eternal life—investing our hearts, time, and energy into pleasing God. Jesus was all about building God's kingdom, a vision we should share if we are to have an extraordinary, abundant life.

Find Your Mission

Just as Jesus was passionate about His mission, we need to be passionate about ours. In the Gospels, we see Jesus living His life through the filter of God's will. Like Jesus, we should live life through the filter of God's Word and His purpose for our lives. Our decisions should be based on what will further God's kingdom and what will please our Father in heaven. Unfortunately, we often make decisions based on personal desires, with no conscious thought of God and His will. Worse yet, sometimes we know what God would have us do, but it's inconvenient for us, or we just don't want to do it. Jesus' entire life was an inconvenience for Him. Why should ours be any different? Those times when we know what we should do to please God, but decide to please ourselves, are significant. If we know the good we ought to do, we should do it. It pleases God and keeps us from sin.

It's true that living for God is often inconvenient, but that inconvenience leads to great joy and spiritual growth. Years ago, my husband's friend decided to give his life to Christ. At the time, he was attending college about three hours from our home.

It certainly would have been more convenient if my husband suggested to him that he come home the next weekend and be baptized at the church building. It would have been convenient for my husband, but God's will and building His kingdom were the priorities. He got in his car with another friend, drove to the college, found a pool, and baptized him that day. Afterward, they all went out to celebrate the new birth and addition of a brother in Christ. My husband knew the good he ought to do and did it — God's will came first.

Service to God never ends in regret. If we keep our focus on doing God's will, we will have many remarkable experiences. Remember, when we are doing God's will, we are working alongside Him and get front row seats to see Him work.

There is a lot of talk these days, in and out of the church, about man's purpose. Rick Warren's book, *The Purpose Driven Life*, has sold millions of copies proving people are hungry to know why they're here. As Christians, we are fortunate to know our purpose. When we became Christians, we took on Christ's purpose as our own. However, we often struggle with tour purpose, thinking God must have something more for us to do. Though we all share the same purpose, God calls each of us to fulfill that purpose in a variety of ways. God has gifted each of us in different ways, but God means for us to use those gifts to achieve our over-arching purpose of doing His will and accomplishing His work (1 Peter 4:10). If we are truly to be like Christ, God's will must come before anything else in our lives. Even more, it must be what feeds our souls, as doing the will of God fed Christ's.

Walk the Walk

Our passion for following Christ will be clear to others by what we say and do. You've heard it said that someone "lives, eats, and breathes" something. Some people live, eat, and breathe a hobby, work, or even a relationship. A Christian is to live, eat, and breathe Christ. Jesus talks about this in John 17, when He is praying in the garden before His arrest. This is one of the most beautiful passages and prayers in Scripture. Take a minute and go read for yourself what Christ prays for you in John 17:20-23.

Isn't it amazing to know that Jesus prayed for you and all those who follow Him? He prayed for us to be in Him and for Him to be in us. As Christians, we are one with Christ and with God. In Acts 17, Paul was speaking to the Athenians, proclaiming to them who the "unknown God" is to whom they had erected an altar. In his discourse, Paul says in Acts 17:28, "for in Him we live and move and exist, as even some of your own poets have said, 'For we also are His children.'" In Him we live, move, and exist. *Who* we are is determined by *Whose* we are. We belong to God through the blood of Jesus Christ, and it is in Him that we live, move, and exist. Paul says in 1 Corinthians 6:17 that "But the one who joins himself to the Lord is one spirit with Him." Who we are is so intertwined with Jesus that we cannot define who we are without Him. We are one with Him.

I'd like us to look at one last passage. Read Psalm 63:1-8. David's voice is filled with love, longing, and faith. Let's notice two things about David's desires. First, his desire is for God, *not for what God can do for him*. If we want to be all in for God, we must desire a close relationship — a oneness —with Him. Second, David places the right priority on that relationship. He longs for God above all else. He says his soul clings to Him, and God's love is better than life. God is always on his mind, even through the night.

As God's children, we should have that same longing for closeness with God that only He can satisfy. If we possess that passion, the passion we had when we first became Christians, non-Christians will be attracted to the Lord through us, and Christians will be encouraged in their faith. Spending time with a new Christian always feels like a breath of fresh air to me. It reminds me of the eagerness and determination I had all those years ago, reigniting my faith, making me a much better ambassador for Christ and determined to put God and His will above everything.

Having that passion expresses itself in another way we haven't discussed yet. It expresses itself through suffering. Jesus knew this expression of passion well. In 2004, Mel Gibson produced a movie that touched millions: *The Passion of the Christ*. The passion referenced in the title is the suffering Christ endured the last week of His life through the crucifixion. His entire life was marked by His devotion to doing God's will and being about His business. That devotion extended to, and expressed itself in, obedience to suffering and eventually death on the cross. Jesus knew God's plan. He knew the suffering God called Him to endure. He understood the sacrifice He was to make for the sins of mankind, for our sins. He willingly suffered on our behalf because He knew it was necessary.

We have all heard and shared that Jesus suffered and sacrificed Himself to save us. When we say this, it is often without feeling and more of a factual statement. The ability to state it in such a matter-of-fact manner could be because we tend to forget that Jesus was human. We need to remind ourselves of Jesus' humanity. Sometimes, we are so focused on the divinity of Jesus that we gloss over His humanity. But His humanity brings His suffering and sacrifice to life and pierces the heart. Take in Jesus' humanity on the night He was arrested.

They went to a place called Gethsemane, and Jesus said to his
disciples, "Sit here while I pray." He took Peter, James and John
along with him, and he began to be deeply distressed and troubled.
"My soul is overwhelmed with sorrow to the point of death," he said
to them. "Stay here and keep watch." He withdrew about a stone's
throw beyond them, knelt down and prayed, "Father, if you are
willing, take this cup from me; yet not my will, but yours be done."
An angel from heaven appeared to him and strengthened him. And
being in anguish, he prayed more earnestly, and his sweat was like
drops of blood falling to the ground.

When he rose from prayer and went back to the disciples, he found
them asleep, exhausted from sorrow.

"Couldn't you men keep watch with me for one hour?" he asked
Peter. "Watch and pray so that you will not fall into temptation. The
spirit is willing, but the flesh is weak."

He went away a second time and prayed, "My Father, if it is not
possible for this cup to be taken away unless I drink it, may your
will be done."

When he came back, he again found them sleeping, because their
eyes were heavy. So he left them and went away once more and
prayed the third time, saying the same thing.

Then he returned to the disciples and said to them, "Are you still
sleeping and resting? Look, the hour has come, and the Son of
Man is delivered into the hands of sinners. Rise! Let us go! Here
comes my betrayer!"

(Mark 14:32-34; Luke 22:41-45; Matthew 26:40b-46, NIV)

Fully Divine, Fully Human

Jesus' humanity was on full display in the garden. He was overwhelmed to the point of death. In the midst of His terror and
sorrow, Jesus knew the person to turn to was God, His Father.

He prayed, pleading for God to remove the cup of suffering that He knew He must drink. He pleaded, but He also submitted to God by saying, "not my will, but yours be done." He was in such a state that an angel came to strengthen Him, yet Jesus continued to pray, "not my will, but yours." Even in this situation, when He is overcome with sorrow, His desire is to do the will of God. If it is God's will for Him to suffer and die on the cross, then He will do it, willingly giving up His life for us.

When someone buys us a birthday gift, we reciprocate their kindness by purchasing them a gift on their birthday. Whenever someone has us over for dinner, we reciprocate by opening our home to them for a meal. We know what to do when someone does something nice for us, but what do we do when someone has chosen to lay down His life for us? What is the correct response to that? Jesus chose to lay down His life for us, and as His disciples, our response should be to lay down our lives for Him. In Mark 8:31-33, Jesus speaks plainly of the suffering He must endure, His death, and resurrection. Peter gets upset, and Scripture records he "began to rebuke Him." Jesus responds to Peter by saying, "Get behind Me, Satan; for you are not setting your mind on God's interests, but man's." He wanted Peter to put God's will above his own desires. In verses 34-35, Scripture says, "And He summoned the crowd with His disciples, and said to them, 'If anyone wishes to come after Me, he must deny himself, and take up his cross and follow Me. For whoever wishes to save his life will lose it, but whoever loses his life for My sake and the gospel's will save it.'" There it is. The proper response to Jesus' sacrificing His life for us is to take up our cross and follow Him. We must willingly give up our lives for Him and the gospel to save others.

Taking up our cross daily, in a practical sense, means responding to the text message that wakes you at three in the morning from someone in need. It means changing your plans at a moment's notice because someone else's need is greater than yours. It means opening your home for someone who needs a place to stay, knowing the inconvenience it will cause you. It means spending time with people in prayer or in Bible study, knowing you have a million other things to do. It means expecting and accepting the ridicule you receive from others because of your faith in Jesus. It means accepting the rejection you will experience when sharing the gospel with others, even from those closest to you. It may mean turning down that promotion at work because, though it would benefit you financially, it would demand too much time—time better spent in service of the Lord. For some, it even means putting your life in danger in a foreign country to spread the good news of salvation through Jesus Christ. To boil it all down, taking up our cross daily is doing God's will, not ours. It's being Jesus to whoever needs Him.

When reading the book of Acts, we see the persecution and suffering the church experienced. When God sent Ananias to Paul, He told Ananias, "I will show him how much he must suffer for My name's sake" (Acts 9:16). This same Paul, who is no stranger to suffering for Christ, writes in Philippians 1:29, "For to you it has been granted for Christ's sake, not only to believe in Him, but also to suffer for His sake." Paul makes it sound like a wish fulfilled or a gift. Now that's a new twist on suffering. I think James learned a similar lesson, because he writes in James 1:2, "Consider it all joy, my brethren, when you encounter various trials..." So, the question becomes, knowing we will suffer for following Jesus, how do we do that with the joy James writes about? The same way Jesus did. In Hebrews 12:1b-3, we read, "Let us also lay aside every encumbrance and the sin which so easily entangles us, and let us run with endurance the race that is set before us, fixing our eyes on Jesus, the author and perfecter of faith, who **for the joy set before Him** endured the cross, despising the shame, and has sat down at the right hand of the throne of God. For consider Him who has endured such hostility by sinners against Himself, so that you will not grow weary and lose heart." *(emphasis mine)*

The Hebrews writer tells us to keep our eyes on Jesus, then tells us what we'll see if we focus on Him. Jesus endured the cross for the "joy set before him." The joy Jesus focused on was being obedient to God, doing His will and then sitting at His right hand. He knew what He had to look forward to and that it was worth more than life itself. When we focus on Jesus, we see what He endured, how He suffered, and we receive strength and encouragement from Him.

God's Spirit and power will hold us up through any suffering we experience. Jesus is still our example, and it's because of Him that we must not give up. Hebrews 12:4 says, "You have not yet resisted to the point of shedding blood in your striving against sin." It is as if the writer is saying, "Put this in perspective. What you're going through is nothing compared to what Christ went through for you." Jesus gave everything for us. He never gave up or gave in. So, stay strong, don't give in to sin; be obedient to the will of God. We have the same joy set before us that Jesus did — the joy of obedience, which results in eternal life with the Lord. When you feel you're suffering or being persecuted for your faith, let that joy fuel your passion for living for Christ and doing God's will.

Remember how it felt all those years ago to be all in for Jesus. It doesn't have to be a memory. You can get up every morning excited about working alongside God and looking for the opportunities He provides. Forget the mundane, ordinary life you may have been living. It's time to live an extraordinary life. Grab onto it; it's there for the taking. Walk in obedience to God's will and finish the work He has for you. Take hold of life and live it to the fullest, because that is why Jesus came.

....

Bold Points to Ponder

- Do you know someone who lives life to the fullest, holding nothing back?

- Jesus lived a full life because He was passionate about His purpose. Jesus is our example, so what should our passion be?

  - Read Romans 12:1,2 and Colossians 1:9. How do you know what God's will is?

- Read the following verses and write down what you learn about living a full, abundant, and extraordinary life.

  Matthew 6:33,34 _____

  Philippians 4:13 _____

  Psalm 37:4 _____

  John 8:12 _____

  Psalm 16:11 _____

  Colossians 3:23,24 _____

  2 Timothy 1:7 _____

- Identify one worldly attitude that has crept into your life without your realizing it. What will you do to correct it?

- What are some things in your life that shift your focus away from your purpose? What can you do to stop yourself from chasing "squirrels?"

- Read James 4:13-17. What does James say about living according to our own desires? What does the Scripture say concerning choosing our will rather than God's?

- Read the following scriptures. What does Jesus say about His suffering in each?

Luke 22:15 _____

Luke 17:25 _____

Luke 24:26 _____

- Read Mark 14:32-34; Luke 22:41-45; Matthew 26:40b-46. List the ways you see Jesus' humanity in the garden.

- What does taking up your cross and following Jesus mean to you? What does it look like? How do you do it?

9

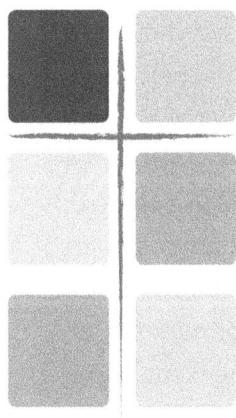

Obedient to the Spirit

A runner who hasn't properly hydrated on a hot day will not get far. A campfire constructed with damp wood will not burn for long. A car running on empty will soon come to a stop. A cellphone with no charge is useless. These are just a few examples of things unable to function without their needed fuel. We understand this about our bodies and see that we feed them. We understand the need to power up certain things like phone and cars. Why then do we find it difficult to apply this same concept to our spiritual lives?

We have been discussing being passionate about all areas of our lives as Christians. We've discussed the importance of looking like Jesus, being aware of how our lives reflect on the name of Christ, being passionate about the Word of God, doing God's will, and living the extraordinary life Jesus came to give us.

It's great to talk about passion, but from where do we get this passion or zeal? Is it just a matter of willing it? Let me share with you a little story about a frog, a toad, and some cookies.

One day Toad baked some cookies and took them over to his friend Frog's house. They both ate some and agreed they were the best. Soon they realized they had a problem. They could not stop eating the cookies. They tried various ways of keeping themselves from eating them, including tying the cookie box with string and putting it up on a high shelf. Nothing worked; they just didn't have enough willpower. So, Frog came up with a solution. He took the box outside, opened it, and called for the birds to come eat the cookies. In a matter of minutes, all the cookies vanished. This made Toad sad, and he went home to bake a cake, but Frog was happy, saying that now they had lots of willpower.[2] Do you see yourself in Toad and Frog? Unfortunately, I can relate to them. I seem to have a problem with willpower, especially when it concerns chocolate. Willpower is not enough for a lot of things in life. We all try to overcome things by willpower, and many times, we can't do it. It is the same with having passion in our Christian lives — we can will it for a while, pushing ourselves, but eventually, our willpower will not be enough to sustain the passion. We need something more than willpower. So, from where does the zeal for the will of God come? What powers the passionate Christian woman? The answer is the Holy Spirit — He is the source of our power.

When we believed in Jesus Christ, repented of our sins, confessed Him as our Lord and Savior, and were baptized for the forgiveness of sins, we received a free gift from God: the Holy Spirit. The fact that we have the Holy Spirit means that we have power. Not just any power, not your run-of-the-mill willpower—we have the power of God living within us. Ephesians 1:17-19a reveals, "I keep asking that the God of our Lord Jesus

---

2.   Lobel, Arnold. *Frog and Toad Together.* Harcourt Brace & Company ed. Harper Collins, 1972.

Christ, the glorious Father, may give you the Spirit of wisdom and revelation, so that you may know him better. I pray that the eyes of your heart may be enlightened in order that you may know the hope to which he has called you, the riches of his glorious inheritance in his holy people, and his incomparably great power for us who believe" (NIV).

Power of the Spirit

What a power it is! It is the same power God used in raising Jesus from the dead. What a gift to have access to that power every day! In 2 Peter 1:1-3, Scripture tells us that the power of God gives us everything we need for "life and godliness" through the knowledge of Jesus that the Holy Spirit shares with us (1 Corinthians 2:9-13). Why is it that while having such a great power living within us, so many of us are living weak and powerless lives? To answer this question, we need to begin by taking a closer look at this "Spirit of power."

The first thing we should know about the Holy Spirit is that He's a person. Jesus never spoke of Him as "it." Since He is a person, it isn't surprising that Scripture speaks of Him as possessing human qualities. In Ephesians 4:30, we're warned not to grieve the Holy Spirit. How do we "grieve the Holy Spirit?" By the sin Paul lists in verse 31. Sin grieves God and grieves His Holy Spirit living within us. The Holy Spirit knows the thoughts of God because He comes from God (1 Corinthians 2:9-12). One of His purposes is to help us understand God and the unbelievable gift He has given us through the sacrifice of His Son. The Holy Spirit possesses intellect, which means He can reason and share the thoughts of God with us. Back in 2 Timothy 1:7, Paul tells us the Spirit we have is not only one of power, but one of love. He also writes in Romans 5:5 that "the love of God has been poured out within our hearts through the Holy Spirit who was given to us." The Holy Spirit loves and enables us to love others with the love of God. All the above qualities are those of a person, not an "it."

Like Jesus, not only is the Holy Spirit a person, but He is also divine. In Acts 4, Luke writes that the believers who owned land or houses sold them and brought the proceeds of the sales and laid them at the apostles' feet. They then gave the money to those who had a need. Acts 5 recounts the story of a husband and wife by the names of Ananias and Sapphira. They sold some property and laid the money at the feet of the apostles. Unfortunately, Ananias misrepresented his offering. He told them that what he was giving as an offering was the total amount he had received from the sale. In Acts 5:3-4, the Scripture says, "But Peter said, 'Ananias, why has Satan filled your heart to lie to the Holy Spirit and to keep back some of the price of the land? While it remained unsold, did it not remain your own? And after it was sold, was it not under your control? Why is it that you have conceived this deed in your heart? You have not lied to men but to God.'" Notice that God and the Holy Spirit are used interchangeably in these verses. If we lie to the Holy Spirit, we lie to God. The Holy Spirit is divine.

The Holy Spirit is also eternal. Hebrews 9:14 refers to "the eternal Spirit," and we see that the Holy Spirit was present at creation in Genesis 1:2. "The earth was formless and void, and darkness was over the surface of the deep, and the Spirit of God was moving over the surface of the waters." The Holy Spirit was with God the Father and Jesus at the creation of the world, and He is now with us as we live our lives for Christ, empowering us and guiding us every day. Scripture calls Him by different names, each describing a bit of who He is and His purpose. Jesus called Him the Counselor or Helper (John 16:7) and the Spirit of truth (John 16:13). He told the disciples it was for their benefit that He was leaving so that the Spirit could come. Although the disciples did not want Jesus to leave, they would eventually understand the gift He left with them. Jesus may have left physically, but He did not leave the disciples alone, and He has not left us alone. There is no doubt that the Holy Spirit is a person, and He is God living in each of us because we belong to Christ.

We know that Jesus came to earth with a specific mission: to sacrifice His life to save all who believe in Him. His mission was for all people if they would accept Him. The Holy Spirit also came here with a mission. His mission is specific to people who have already put on Jesus as their Lord and Savior. He was sent to Christians. There are a couple of overarching reasons God sends the Spirit to dwell within us. Let's explore them.

When someone is on their deathbed, they will often use their last moments to say things that are important to them. A friend of mine, when he was close to death, used his time to ask the minister visiting him to share the gospel with his unbelieving family members who were sitting with him. He said he wanted to know that they were told about Jesus before he passed on. In the same way, Jesus, knowing He was leaving His disciples and going to be with the Father, spoke an important message to them before He was taken up. In Acts 1:8, Jesus explains, "but you will receive power when the Holy Spirit has come upon you; and you shall be My witnesses both in Jerusalem, and in all Judea and Samaria, and even to the remotest part of the earth." Jesus knew these were to be the last words He would speak to the apostles and chose to leave them with an important message. He told them about the power they would be receiving from the Holy Spirit—power that would enable them to become His witnesses to the world. He gave them a mission and the one thing they needed to accomplish that mission, the Holy Spirit.

A Sacred Mission

The mission Jesus gave the apostles that day is the same mission we share today. Paul says we are Christ's ambassadors. God makes His appeal through us for all people to be reconciled to Him through Jesus (2 Corinthians 5:18-20). When we put on Christ, we accept the important mission to be witnesses and ambassadors for Him, telling people about Jesus, what He did and continues to do. Our purpose is to encourage others to put their faith in Jesus and be reconciled to God, accepting the free gift of eternal life. As Jesus told the apostles, it is the Holy Spirit who empowers and enables us to be His witnesses to the world.

The second main reason the Holy Spirit dwells within us is to guide us and empower us to do all that God has planned for us to do. Paul wrote in Ephesians 2:10, "For we are His workmanship, created in Christ Jesus for good works, which God prepared beforehand so that we would walk in them." God has a purpose or calling for each one of us, and He gives us the Holy Spirit during baptism to help us fulfill that calling. Here is something to consider. When did Jesus' ministry begin? Its official beginning was after the Holy Spirit came down on Him at His baptism. Likewise, Paul's ministry began after his baptism and receiving of the Holy Spirit. Before that, under his own power, he had been sincere in his devotion to God — he had just been sincerely mistaken. After receiving the Holy Spirit, Paul was able to fulfill his calling, no matter the circumstances, through the power the Spirit provided. Our mission, purpose, or calling began the day we came up out of the waters of baptism a new creation in Christ. We did not rise out of the waters alone; we rose with the Holy Spirit living in us, so we would be able to serve God and complete our mission. Like Paul, we need the Holy Spirit to guide us and make us aware of God's calling. It is His power enabling us to accomplish the good works God has prepared for us to do.

The Holy Spirit is not a bystander in our lives. He is active, though we sometimes do not recognize what He is doing. Have you ever felt the gentle nudge of the Spirit? I have. Years ago, I was in the middle of cleaning up a mildly flooded basement, when an old friend of mine kept coming to mind. I was busy but decided I'd try to contact her later. Even after making that decision, I could not stop thinking of her. The feeling that it was God bringing her to mind and that He wanted me to call her led me to leave my mop and head up the stairs. We hadn't spoken in a couple of years. When she answered the phone and heard my voice, she began to cry. She said she couldn't believe I called. It turned out she had been thinking about me and wishing she could talk with me. I asked her what was wrong, and she told me about a miscarriage she'd had earlier in the day. Her husband had to go back to work, and she was all alone and incredibly sad. We spoke for quite a while, and I followed up with her later. I hadn't even known she was pregnant, but God did. The Holy Spirit knew I had a "good work" prepared for me to do that day, and He spurred me on to do it. We must be receptive to His guidance.

We need to be sensitive to the Holy Spirit's leading, but there is one caveat, and it is a serious one. When we believe the Holy Spirit is leading us to do something or say something, before we follow that leading, we need to be sure it is not something contrary to the teaching of Scripture. Let me give you an example. One day I had a woman tell me, after deciding to divorce, that she knew God wanted her to do it. She said that God wanted her to be happy, and since she was not happy with her husband, God would be okay with her divorcing him. She truly believed God was telling her to take this step. Obviously, she was mistaken about God's wishes and was being misled. I spoke with her about how God feels about divorce, showing her what God has to say about it in the Scriptures. Then I asked her why she thought

God wanted her to be happy. I asked her where God promises us happiness in the Bible. She couldn't give me an answer. Then we discussed that true happiness is not a feeling. Instead, it is found in living in obedience to God and His Word. Unfortunately, she didn't change her mind about the divorce.

When we follow a feeling, thought, ideology, or anything else not aligned with God's Word, it is definitely not the Holy Spirit's gentle nudge or whisper to our heart. He will never lead us to do anything contrary to Scripture. It is our responsibility, when thinking God is calling us to do something, to check it against the plumb line of Scripture. If it doesn't line up with God's Word, we will know it is not from God.

What causes our passion for living the Christian life to fizzle? What drains us of the power of the Holy Spirit? Some of the things that come to my mind might be the same as yours: lack of prayer, not spending time in the Word, pride, bitterness, shame, anger, worry, guilt, fear, unconfessed sin, and a lack of trust in God. Any of those things can take the wind out of our sails and send us plunging back to earth. I'm sure you could add many more things to the list, but you get the point. We talked in an earlier chapter about living an extraordinary life in Christ. Christ saved us to soar to the heights with the power of the Holy Spirit. Isaiah 40:31 says, "but those who wait for the LORD will gain new strength; they will mount up with wings like eagles, They will run and not get tired. They will walk and not become weary." God doesn't mean for us to plod through life. He means for us to soar. Trying to soar by our own willpower won't work because that can never last. The only way to soar is by the power of the Holy Spirit.

Let's return to our story of Frog, Toad, and the cookies. As long as they relied on their own willpower to not eat those cookies, they failed. There was only one way to be sure they wouldn't eat them. Frog climbed the ladder, got the box, cut the string, and opened it. He looked at the cookies, took the box outside, and invited the birds to take the cookies away. By doing that, he possessed the power he needed to not eat them because they were no longer under his control. We must have the courage to take the "box" off the shelf and look into it. We need to face whatever areas of our lives we are still trying to control on our own and offer them up to the Lord. It is then that the Holy Spirit can freely do His powerful work in our lives, enabling us to soar like the eagle, while we bring as many along for the ride as possible.

Bold Points to Ponder

- Look back over the previous chapters. Which of the areas discussed do you feel you need to work on most? Why?

  - What is one change you can make to improve in that specific area?

- Think of a time when you relied on "willpower" to accomplish a goal but were not able to sustain the willpower. (Maybe a New Year's resolution?) How long were you able to sustain that willpower? How did you feel when you lost your willpower?

- Read and write out 2 Timothy 1:7.

  - What do you learn about this gift, the Holy Spirit, from in this verse?

- We are not powerless to live the Christian life. Read Ephesians 1:17-20. What do you learn about the Holy Spirit's power from these verses?

- Read each of the following Scriptures and write down what you learn about the Holy Spirit. What human qualities does He possess?

  - Ephesians 4:30-32
  - 1 Corinthians 2:9-13
  - 2 Timothy 1:7
  - Romans 5:5

- What characteristic of the Holy Spirit do you most appreciate and why?

- Look up the following scriptures, and make note of the name given the Holy Spirit in each one and what He does.

  - Ephesians 1:13
  - John 16:13
  - Hebrews 10:29
  - Romans 8:2
  - Romans 8:9
  - 1 Corinthians 3:16

- Read 1 Corinthians 5:18-20. In what ways have you, or can you, be a witness for Christ to the world?

- Do you believe you have personally experienced the guidance or leading of the Holy Spirit? If so, describe the experience and how you responded.

- Read Isaiah 40:29-31. Think of your life. What things are you are holding onto that are preventing you from "soaring" in the kingdom of God? What is one change you can make that will enable you to soar in God's kingdom with the help of the Holy Spirit?

10

Tied to the Truth

've been a Christian since 1980, yet I'm often still surprised by how the Holy Spirit works. A while back, I was in a ladies' retreat planning meeting as we discussed possible speakers. Out of nowhere, a name popped into my head. Immediately, I began holding a conversation in my mind. *I will not say her name. She hates public speaking. There is no way she would want to do it.* You can imagine my surprise when moments later I heard myself suggesting her name to the other ladies. Since I had actually suggested *my best friend*, they tasked me with inviting her to be our speaker. I drove home that day, not believing what I had done and dreading the phone call I would be making that night.

When I called her, I remember telling her she might want to sit down. I told her about the meeting and finally broached the subject of her speaking for us. My question was met with dead silence, (later, I learned she had been sitting on her bed and fell backwards in disbelief) and then she asked if I was joking. I assured her it was a serious offer and that I didn't know how her name escaped out of my mouth at the meeting, because I knew how much she hated public speaking. She asked if she could have a couple of days to think and pray about it, and we hung up the phone. Two days later, she called and agreed to do it. She told me she had recently prayed about feeling the need for more concentrated study of God's Word, and she had expressed this to her husband. As we talked, we both became convinced God was answering her prayer through this offer to speak, which would require intense study time for her. We ended our conversation, amazed once again at the power of the Holy Spirit and the working of God's will.

The Holy Spirit at Work

The Holy Spirit plays many roles in our lives. In fact, we cannot even call ourselves Christians if we don't have Him. He is vital to our salvation. In John 3:5-8, Jesus responds to Nicodemus' question about being born again. In verse 5 He says, "Truly, truly, I say to you, unless one is born of water and the Spirit he cannot enter into the kingdom of God." If anyone wants to enter the kingdom of God, they must be born of the Spirit. Paul drives this point home in Romans 8:9, "But if anyone does not have the Spirit of Christ, he does not belong to Him." Paul doesn't mince words. He states plainly that if the Spirit of Christ does not live in us, we do not belong to Him.

Though the Holy Spirit plays a major role in salvation, His work is far from over when we come up out of the waters of baptism. The Holy Spirit now lives in us, and God expects us to live a new life (we're a new creation - 2 Corinthians 5:17) and no longer live as if our lives are our own. We belong to God because He purchased us with the blood of His Son. However, God knows and understands us. He knows we are weak and cannot turn away from our old lives of sin on our own. To that end, another major role of the Holy Spirit is sanctification.

Sanctification is one of those religious words that people often find difficult to understand. Basically, to sanctify means "to set apart as holy and to free from sin or purify" (Oxford English Dictionary). The Spirit sanctifies us, sets us apart, at the time of baptism and continues the sanctification process throughout our lives. Jesus, in His prayer in John 17:17, prays, "Sanctify them in the truth; Your word is truth." In John 14:16-17, Jesus promises to send a Counselor, the "Spirit of truth." Finally, in John 16:13, Jesus says, "But when He, the Spirit of truth, comes, He will guide you into all the truth; for He will not speak on His own initiative, but whatever He hears, He will speak; and He will disclose to you what is to come."

Let's put these three scriptures together. The truth sanctifies us; Jesus calls the Holy Spirit the Spirit of truth and says He'll guide us into all the truth. God's Word is truth, and the Holy Spirit uses it powerfully in our lives. Using God's Word, He points us to the truth. Do not think the Spirit continues to sanctify us on completely on His own — we have a role to play as well. He opens our eyes to where changes need to be made, and we are the ones who need to make them. We must work hand in hand with the Spirit when He shows us the truth. His power enables us to change our attitudes, our thoughts, and the way we live, so we can better please God. As Jesus said, He guides us.

Something happens as the Holy Spirit continues to sanctify us. A change takes place. Romans 12:2 tells us not to be like the world anymore, but to be "transformed by the renewing of your mind." How does this mind renewal occur? it happens through the Holy Spirit. He uses the Word of God to open our eyes, so we can see the sinful attitudes and thoughts and replace them with godly ones. The Bible gives us plenty of examples of the transforming work of the Spirit, but perhaps there is none better than the transformation of Peter.

Peter loved Jesus, but it seems he was a big talker. He told Jesus He would die with him. Jesus responded that he would deny Him three times. Peter said, "No, never." On the night of Jesus' arrest, Peter couldn't even stay awake while Jesus prayed. Oh, there was a glimmer of Peter's desire to fight for the Lord when he took off Malchus' ear with his sword, but that quickly passed. As the night wore on, Peter did, indeed, deny knowing Jesus three times. After his denial and Jesus' crucifixion, Peter was a broken and defeated man. After the resurrection, Jesus forgave Peter, but you can bet that Peter was having trouble forgiving himself. When Jesus told the disciples to wait in Jerusalem for the Spirit to come, Peter was among them. Just as Jesus promised, He sent the Holy Spirit to them. The Spirit filled them and came upon them, and an unbelievable transformation came over Peter. Boldness replaced fear and timidity. Peter was the leader of the disciples, preached on Pentecost to thousands and continued to preach — refusing to back down even in the face of personal danger and death. The Spirit gave him the strength and courage to speak the gospel with boldness and confidence, something just a couple of months before seemed impossible. This man who said, "I don't know Him" three times out of fear, began proclaiming as loudly as he could, to as many as possible, "I know Him. I love Him. I serve Him. He is Lord and Savior. Repent!" Now that's a transformation.

We see the Holy Spirit at work throughout the entire book of Acts, and we see His fingerprints all over the entire New Testament. This Spirit, who was in the transformation business in the first century, continues transforming people today. He is alive in every Christian, still leading us into truth, guiding us, comforting us, interceding for us, and teaching us how to live.

The Holy Spirit not only teaches us, but He reminds us of the Word. He still speaks the words of God to us today, so we can speak them to others. Let me tell you a story. It's something that happened to me as a new Christian and convinced me the Holy Spirit is real and active today. He is present and leads us into truth.

This occurred before my husband, Mark, and I were married. I was a new Christian, and he was not yet a Christian. We were at a party, and he knew I'd been reading the Bible and that I'd given my life to Christ, so he was asking me many questions. As a lot of non-Christians will do, they try to find the one question that will stump you, to be able to say, "See. You don't even know." So, he said to me, "All right, answer this one for me. Where did Satan come from?" I stood there for a second and shot up a quick prayer, asking God to give me the answer. Then I said, "Well, he was originally an angel, and he wanted to take the place of God, to be greater than God, and he got thrown out of heaven." "Okay," he said, "tell me where that is in the Bible." So, I prayed again. "God, this is important. I really need the answer." Then I said to Mark, "Isaiah 14:12-14." He said, "Are you sure?" I said, "Yes." The truth is, I wasn't sure. I had never opened the book of Isaiah in my life and couldn't wait to get home to look it up. When I got home later that night, I ran upstairs to my room, pulled out my Bible — I had to look for Isaiah in the Bible because I did not know where it was — looked it up, read it, and was amazed. I remember saying, "Oh, God, You are good." I was so relieved, because I knew Mark would go home and look it up. He wasn't just going to believe what I said; he would verify it. My only explanation for what took place that night is the Holy Spirit. God knew how important that question was, how important it was to have that answer, and He gave it to me. I'm convinced that the Holy Spirit is at work in us today. He is active. He will give us the words we need to reach others. He will point us to the truth, but we must trust Him to do it. We must believe He will do it.

Life in the Holy Spirit

Saying we believe in the Holy Spirit, and everything the Bible says about Him, is easy. Living like we believe it, is another story. When we first become Christians, we feel like the Holy Spirit is so active in our lives. We see evidence of Him at work in us and around us all the time. If only we could hold on to that belief and experience. One thing that affects our zeal about the Holy Spirit is the way He's treated or talked about in the church. Think back over all the sermons you've heard and all the classes you've been in since your baptism. How many have been about the Holy Spirit? Throughout the New Testament, we see how active the Holy Spirit is. He is vital to the health of the Christians and to the church, and He remains just as vital today. Yet, we hardly speak of Him to each other or in our churches. We know He lives in us, but we live as though we only find Him in the pages of Scripture. Living this way prevents us from experiencing His power.

I know of some women who have built "She Sheds" in their backyards — one as a place to write undisturbed and another for her crafting. (I admit to dreaming about having one myself for a writing studio or for my crafts, but that is not going to happen.) Imagine if these ladies went out to their sheds, flipped on the light switch, and nothing happened. Upon some inspection, they realized not only were they not hooked into the power grid, but they had forgotten to put in the electrical wiring. They would be standing in their beautiful new She Sheds without the ability to accomplish anything because there was no power. You would never build a She Shed or house like that, and God doesn't build His house, the church, that way either.

God builds the church with individuals who each have the Holy Spirit and His power living within them. First Corinthians 6:19 says, "Or do you not know that your body is a temple of the Holy Spirit who is in you, whom you have from God, and that you are not your own?" The Holy Spirit lives in us and Paul tells us in Ephesians 1:18-20 that the power of the Spirit living in us is the same power that raised Jesus from the dead. With so much power living in us, why do we so often feel powerless? Those powerless times come from not plugging into the power source, the Spirit. If we did, the light of the Spirit would shine through us to the world. Ephesians 5:8-10 teaches, "for you were formerly darkness, but now you are Light in the Lord; walk as children of Light (for the fruit of the Light consists in all goodness and right-eousness and truth), trying to learn what is pleasing to the Lord."

As verse 10 commands, we must find out what pleases the Lord and then live that way. By doing so, God's light will shine through us to the world. With the Spirit living in us, we have all the power we need to be the light to the world. The bad news is that many of us aren't sure how to connect with that power.

There are some misconceptions out there about the Holy Spirit. You've probably heard of someone praying for more of the Holy Spirit. Maybe you've done so yourself. Where does that idea come from? Acts 2:38 says, "Peter replied, 'Repent and be baptized, each of you, in the name of Jesus Christ for the forgiveness of your sins, and you will receive the gift of the Holy Spirit.'" Peter didn't say you'll receive part of the Holy Spirit. He said you will receive the Holy Spirit. God is not slicing up the Spirit and giving us just a portion or two. He gives us His Spirit completely. The Spirit gives us different gifts, but we all have the same Spirit (1 Corinthians 12:4). Therefore, it makes little sense to pray for more of the Spirit. Perhaps people are getting the idea from something Paul wrote in Ephesians 5:17-18: "So then do not be foolish, but understand what the will of the Lord is. And do not get drunk with wine, for that is dissipation, but be filled with the Spirit." It is the Lord's will that we be filled by the Spirit. It is actually a command. But what does it mean?

Filled with the Spirit

We received the Holy Spirit during baptism. At the risk of sounding like Nicodemus, we can't receive the Spirit again if we already have Him. So, what is God telling us here? If we look at the first part of verse 18, we see the command not to get drunk on wine. We know what someone looks and acts like when they are drunk because they can't hide it. It is clear to all that they are under the influence of alcohol. How does this relate to the filling of the Holy Spirit? When we're filled with the Holy Spirit, we are under His influence, and we won't be able to hide it. People will see the Holy Spirit at work in us. They may not recognize or understand that it is the Holy Spirit, but they will know there is something different about us.

If you think about the Christian women in your life, I'm sure you can think of at least one whom you believe is filled with the Holy Spirit based on what you see in her life. The fruit of the Holy Spirit is evident to all. Still, the command in verse 18 to be filled with the Spirit can be confusing. Ephesians 1:14 describes the Holy Spirit as "a deposit guaranteeing our inheritance" (NIV); since we already have His indwelling, we cannot receive Him again. However, just because we have Him living in us does not mean we are filled with Him. We are told in 1 Thessalonians 5:19 not to "quench the Spirit." This means we can stop the work of the Holy Spirit in our lives, and being involved in sin is one way we do this. Though we have the Holy Spirit, we still struggle with sin in our lives. We get tangled up in things that interfere with us living a Spirit-filled life. God knows of our human weaknesses, and I believe that is why He told us to be filled with the Spirit. Being filled with the Spirit simply means giving control of our lives over to Him.

How do we obey this command? First, we pray and ask God to fill us to overflowing with His Spirit. We know from Ephesians 5:18 that this is God's will, but He will never force us into anything. We must really want to be filled. We must hunger and thirst for righteousness to be filled (Matthew 5:6). We also know from 1 John 5:14-15 that if we ask anything according to God's will, He will give us what we request. So, when we pray, asking God to fill us with His Spirit, we are asking for something we know to be His will, and as a result, we know that He has answered that prayer for us. Our prayer doesn't end there. Let me give you an illustration: I hand you a glass half-filled with lemonade and tell you I would like it to be filled with milk. You would probably think I was a little crazy. Your first thought might be, *Yuck! Mixing lemonade with milk will taste terrible.* You'd be right. However, after you thought for a minute, you'd probably pour the lemonade down the drain and then fill the glass with milk. This is what we need to do when asking God to fill us with the Spirit. We must get ourselves out of the way, pour ourselves down the drain so to speak, so the Spirit can fill us up. This requires us to continually, every day, yield control of our lives to God.

At baptism, we gave God control of our lives, becoming His slaves. As we grow in Christ, the Spirit shines a light on different areas of our lives requiring change — illuminating sin in our lives we often don't know is there. This is a lifelong process, because as long as we are living on the earth, we will struggle with self vs. God. With each new day, we must ask God to control our lives, guide our steps, show us His will, and fill us to overflowing with His Spirit. The truth is, being filled with the Spirit doesn't mean having more of Him; it means having less of ourselves. Paul refers to this in 2 Corinthians 3:17-18 where he says, "Now the Lord is the Spirit, and where the Spirit of the Lord is, there is liberty. But we all, with unveiled face, beholding as in a mirror the glory of the Lord, are being transformed into the same image from glory to glory, just as from the Lord, the Spirit." When Paul says we are being transformed into the same image, he is speaking of the image of the Lord. It is an ongoing process. We will become more and more like Christ, shining forth His glory, as we continue to walk with Him, and it is the Spirit who makes it happen.

The next step in living a Spirit-filled life requires a daily diet of the Word of God. Hebrews 4:12 tells us that the Word of God is alive and sharper than any sword. It's able to "judge the thoughts and intentions of the heart." And 2 Timothy 3:16 says, "All Scripture is inspired by God and profitable for teaching, for reproof, for correction, for training in righteousness." The Holy Spirit is everywhere in the Bible because He inspired its writing. Through the Word of God, the Spirit speaks to us, teaching us how to live the Christian life. He will guide us in our everyday lives, but He also teaches us and corrects us through God's Word. A young couple I know were living together and thought nothing of it. After all, it is a common occurrence in today's culture. To prepare for marriage, they were involved in a Bible study. In the study, they read the Scriptures as part of their homework and were shocked to discover that God did not approve of their living situation. They had not known what they were doing was sinful. The Word of God, inspired by the Holy Spirit, opened their eyes to their sin, and they made the necessary changes to be in obedience to Him. Making changes when faced with the Word of God is not easy. Change is never easy, especially when you are being asked to give up something you enjoy, but they willingly made the change. These young people did what each of us as Christians should do all the time. When reading the Bible, we need to allow the Spirit to show us where our lives are out of step with God's Word, then make whatever changes are necessary to be in obedience to God.

The third step is to pray for God to increase our faith, so we can better discern what holds us back from being filled with the Spirit. In Luke 17:5, the apostles asked Jesus to increase their faith. In Mark 9, a father brings his son who is possessed by an evil spirit to Jesus for healing. The father requests for Jesus to do something for him if He can. Jesus responds that everything is possible for those who believe. I love the father's response. He says, "I do believe; help my unbelief!" (Mark 9:24). Like this father, we must humble ourselves and ask God to increase our faith and help us see what the Spirit wants us to see.

So, to be filled with the Spirit, we should ask God to fill us with His Spirit and offer our lives to Him daily — holding nothing back. We need to be in the Word daily, so the Spirit can speak to us, convict us of sin and teach us the ways of God; and we should pray for an increase of our faith. God is faithful. He will answer our prayers and continue to transform us into the likeness of His Son as long as we are willing.

Through the saving grace of Jesus Christ and the power of the Holy Spirit, we can live a Spirit-filled life as we journey on this earth waiting for Christ's return. Galatians 5:22-25 talks about the fruit of the Spirit. This fruit is a by-product of living under the control of the Spirit: "The fruit of the Spirit is love, joy, peace, patience, kindness, goodness, faithfulness, gentleness, self-control; against such things there is no law. Now those who belong to Christ Jesus have crucified the flesh with its passions and desires.

If we live by the Spirit, let us also walk by the Spirit." **Being filled with the Spirit means we will be transformed to look more like Christ all the time, and the Spirit's fruit will become more evident in our lives. We won't manifest these qualities overnight, but the more we yield control of our lives to God, the more people will see these qualities in us. The Spirit gives us life — let's walk in lockstep with Him, stay close to Him and give every part of ourselves over to His purposes.**

Bold Points to Ponder

- Based on your reading of the previous chapter, list three characteristics of the Holy Spirit.

- Read John 17:17; John 14:16-17; John 16:13. Summarize what these verses tell you about the sanctifying work of the Holy Spirit.

- Read 2 Corinthians 5:17, Galatians 2:20, and Ephesians 2:4-7. What do these verses say to you concerning your life in Christ and how has your life changed since you became that new creation in Christ ?

- Read Romans 6:1-6, 10-14, and Romans 8:1-6, 12-14. According to these verses what happens during baptism?

- These verses help us to know how to overcome sin and live more like Christ. Read 1 Timothy 6:11-14, 2 Timothy 2:22 and James 4:7-8.

  - What are some things from which we should "flee" and what should we pursue instead?

- Write out John 14:26 and Mark 13:11. Put these verses together. What conclusion can you draw from them?

- Read Luke 12:11-12 and Matthew 10:19-20. Describe a time when the Holy Spirit gave you just the right words and/or scriptures you needed when sharing your faith with someone.

  - Did you recognize the Spirit's help? When? Was it during or after the occasion?

  - How did you feel?

- Read Matthew 5:14-16. We all want to shine our lights for the Lord. We also need to be aware of how we might be hiding our light. In what ways do you sometimes hide your light?

- Read Ephesians 5:17-18. What do you think God means when He commands us to "be filled with the Spirit?"

- Read Romans 12:1-2. What is the significance of being a living sacrifice in light of being filled with the Holy Spirit?

11

Inspired to Worship

I n summers past, every Friday morning I would wake up to *Good Morning America* and become a witness to worship. No, not the worship we think of and are a part of on Sunday mornings, but worship nonetheless. Each Friday in the summer, *Good Morning America* presents a concert in Bryant Park in New York City. Invariably, there are several hundred to a couple of thousand people there to watch the musical act. They come dressed like the performers. They scream, shout, sing along with them, jump up and down to the music, carry signs professing undying love for them, and are full of excitement and enthusiasm. There is no doubt; they are worshiping.

As Christians, we are called to worship God. A. W. Tozer said in the book *Worship: The Reason We Were Created*, "Jesus was born of a virgin, suffered under Pontius Pilate, died on the cross and rose from the grave to make worshipers out of rebels!" Before we gave our lives to Christ, we were rebels. We lived to make ourselves happy and fulfill our own desires. For teens and those of college age, success was measured by popularity, the sorority you pledged, or who you were dating. As adults, the size of our house, our occupation, or the kind of car we drove measured our success among other things. These are just a few measures of success, but all measures had the same thing in common: They were all about what made us feel good and what made us look good to others. Our thoughts, as rebels, were far from our Creator and pleasing Him. Rebels don't worship God, they worship themselves.

Need to Worship

The need to worship is one thing that all human beings have in common. Left to our own devices, we search for and find something or someone to worship. Think about our society for a few minutes, and you will no doubt be able to identify different objects people worship today. People worship things like money, material possessions, nature, angels, food, coffee, and probably the most pervasive object of worship today — self. We devote entire industries to the worship of self. Think about the cosmetic industry, the cosmetic surgery industry, and the fitness industry. People spend billions of dollars each year in search of the "perfect" face or body, thinking it will give them the happiness they so desire in life.

Our need to worship is so strong that we will even worship people. This can be dangerous. Many cults have arisen out of people's need to worship. Charles Manson started his own cult called the "Manson Family," a group responsible for the murders of nine people among other crimes. There are others like the Mormons, Moonies, the followers of Jim Jones, and even a man in Florida—José Luis de Jesus Miranda—who claimed to be Jesus come back to earth, as well as the anti-Christ and the apostle Paul. He had a loyal following until his death in 2013. People want something or someone to worship.

The Bible gives us some examples of even Christians who fall down in worship when they shouldn't. Revelation 22:7-9 is one such example. It begins with Jesus saying, "And behold, I am coming quickly. Blessed is he who heeds the words of the prophecy of this book." Then we see John's response beginning in verse 8: "I, John, am the one who heard and saw these things. And when I heard and saw, I fell down to worship at the feet of the angel who showed me these things. But he said to me, 'Do not do that. I am a fellow servant of yours and of your brethren the prophets and of those who heed the words of this book. Worship God.'" John, the "beloved disciple," fell at the feet of an angel to worship him and was rebuked. Christians are not immune to falling into the trap of worshiping something other than God. It is something we must guard against.

Understanding that we have this need to worship requires that we answer the following question: What is *worship*? If you thought of things like singing, praying, and studying the Bible, those are great answers, but they are really actions taken to *express* worship. So, the question remains, what is *worship*? Revelation 4:9-11 says, "And when the living creatures give glory and honor and thanks to Him who sits on the throne, to Him who lives forever and ever, the twenty-four elders will fall down before Him who sits on the throne, and will worship Him who lives forever and ever, and will cast their crowns before the throne, saying, 'Worthy are You, our Lord and our God, to receive glory and honor and power; for You created all things, and because of Your will they existed, and were created.'"

God has provided such a beautiful picture of worship for us in His Word. From this Scripture, we see that *worship* is recognizing who we are in relation to God and acknowledging that He deserves all glory, honor, and praise because it is He who created us and everything else. Out of this recognition and acknowledgment come action. James Pittman in his book, *What Is Worship?* writes, "Worship is the attitude of reverence and adoration, as well as the action of humble, loving service to the God who is worthy." Clearly, worship involves the attitude of the heart that then expresses itself in service to God.

We find the first use of the word *worship* in the Bible in Genesis 22:5. Let me give you a bit of back story first. Abraham and Sarah tried for many years to have children, but were unable to conceive. One day, God promised Abraham that his descendants would be too numerous to count, like sand on the seashore or stars in the heavens. After many more years, when it would be clear it was a miracle of God, Sarah became pregnant. She gave birth to a son, Isaac. God had fulfilled His promise to Abraham. Then in Genesis 22:1-2, Scripture tells us: "Now it came about after these things, that God tested Abraham, and said to him, 'Abraham!' And he said, 'Here I am.' He said, 'Take now your son, your only son, whom you love, Isaac, and go to the land of Moriah, and offer him there as a burnt offering on one of the mountains of which I will tell you.'" It is heart-wrenching to read this story. Imagine how Abraham felt having to live it, how his heart was breaking and the confusion he must have felt. Regardless of his feelings, verse 3 tells us that Abraham got up early the next morning, made preparations for the burnt offering, took along two of his servants and his son, Isaac, and set out for Moriah.

On the third day of their travel, Genesis 22:5-6 says, "Abraham said to his young men, 'Stay here with the donkey, and I and the lad will go over there; and we will worship and return to you.' Abraham took the wood of the burnt offering and laid it on Isaac his son, and he took in his hand the fire and the knife. So the two of them walked on together." During their walk, Isaac asks his father where the lamb for the sacrifice is. Abraham just replies that God will provide it. Let's pick back up in Genesis 22:9, "Then they came to the place of which God had told him; and Abraham built the altar there and arranged the wood, and bound his son Isaac and laid him on the altar, on top of the wood." Thankfully, we all know how the story ends. An angel stops Abraham just in time to save Isaac's life. God does indeed provide the animal for the offering and fulfills His promise of Abraham having a multitude of descendants.

Now take a minute to think about this. God had promised Abraham a son, and He had fulfilled that promise. Abraham dearly loved that boy; Isaac was his heart. God then commanded him to offer him as a burnt offering, and Abraham obeyed. He bound his son, his heart, and laid him on the altar as an offering. The burnt offering is what Abraham was referencing when he told his servants to wait while he and Isaac went to worship God. What was Abraham putting on that altar in worship to God? His son, his heart. Abraham is a good example of how we are to worship God. First, he was obedient. He knew what God told him to do, and he didn't put it off. He got up early the next morning and set out to do the unthinkable because He put God above all else. Second, Abraham was willing to sacrifice what was most dear to him. We, like Abraham, must willingly put our hearts on the altar and sacrifice them to God. God no longer requires burnt offerings; He requires something much more valuable from us — our hearts.

Put Your Heart in It

Worship without involvement of the heart has no meaning. Jesus says, in Matthew 15:8, "This people honors me with their lips, but their heart is far away from me." Jesus does not want us just going through the motions. Instead, He wants us to worship Him with our hearts and serve Him faithfully. He says in Mark 12:30, "Love the Lord your God with all your heart and with all your soul and with all your mind and with all your strength" (NIV). It is out of our love for God that we worship Him and serve Him.

When I returned home following my baptism, I wrote in my journal, telling Jesus how much I loved Him and thanking Him for saving me. I vowed to love Him and serve Him for the rest of my life—and I meant it. For a while, it was fairly easy. With each situation that came up, I asked myself what Jesus would want me to do, or say, or how He would want me to act, and that's what I did. I praised Him in prayer, worshiped Him, and felt in sync with Him. I was excited to live out my faith daily. There is nothing like being a new Christian, full of love, excitement, and zeal. The passion to be like Jesus colors everything we do and say. But over time, gray rises to the surface. We say we are His. We pray, thanking Him for saving us and giving Him praise, but soon after saying "Amen," we go out searching for ways to make ourselves happy, with hardly a thought as to what God may think.

God wants our hearts, and He wants faith and a heart for Him to drive our actions. Let's look at the first recorded act of worship. In Genesis 4:1-7, we see Eve giving birth to Cain and Abel. When they grew, Abel became a shepherd, and Cain became a farmer. It came time for them to worship God by giving Him an offering, and each man brought their offerings to the Lord. Let's pick up in verse 3 and read through verse 7. "In the course of time Cain presented some of the land's produce as an offering to the LORD. And Abel also presented an offering—some of the firstborn of his flock and their fat portions. The LORD had regard for Abel and his offering, but he did not have regard for Cain and his offering. Cain was furious, and he looked despondent. Then the LORD said to Cain, 'Why are you furious? And why do you look despondent? If you do what is right, won't you be accepted? But if you do not do what is right, sin is crouching at the door. Its desire is for you, but you must rule over it'" (CSB). The warning God gave to Cain, to do what is right, is a warning we must all take seriously. If we ignore it, sin will grow in our lives and put a barrier between us and God. Unfortunately, Cain did not heed God's warning and sin grew in his life, culminating in his murdering his brother, Abel.

So, we come to the age-old question of why God accepted Abel's offering and not Cain's. There are a few theories in answer to the question. One theory is that God required a blood sacrifice, which Cain did not bring. However, nowhere in the story does the Scripture say this was a sin offering. Sin offerings require the shedding of blood, which is why Jesus had to shed His blood for us. There are other offerings where animal sacrifice is not required. Though the Scripture doesn't tell us, it is possible that God had previously given them instructions about this offering. Another theory is that Abel offered the better sacrifice. Scripture tells us that Cain offered "some" of the fruits of the soil to the Lord. Abel's offering was some of the firstborn of his flock along with their fat portions. Cain offered some, and Abel offered the best portions of the firstborn of his flock. Cain's offering seemed to be more careless. Unlike Abel, Cain did not give his best to God. This theory could be true and the reason God did not accept Cain's offering. But let's dig a little deeper.

When looking at the two offerings, the real difference is seen in the attitude of the heart. God does not judge one offering better than another based on the object given. Because God looks at the heart, we are all equal. Social status, money, accomplishments — none of that matters. God looks at our hearts. No one is better than another. We see this in Mark 12:41-44, when Jesus praises the offering of the widow who put only a fraction of a penny into the temple treasury. Jesus looked at her heart and knew she had given all she had. She gave everything to God. Her offering required a lot of faith and trust in God that he would meet her needs. Her heart was pure and obedient to God. I believe this was the difference between Cain and Abel.

In Hebrews 11:4, Scripture says, "By faith Abel offered to God a better sacrifice than Cain, through which he obtained the testimony that he was righteous, God testifying about his gifts, and through faith, though he is dead, he still speaks." Abel's offering was made by faith. He brought fat portions of some of the firstborn of his flock. He sacrificed the best of the firstborn with no guarantee there would be more born. Abel's sacrifice showed his faith that God would provide. By inference, Cain's offering lacked faith—he was just going through the motions, performing a duty. He did not bring the firstfruits of his crops, only a portion. It appears Abel's heart was in his offering, but Cain was performing his sacrifice out of obligation, giving "lip service" as Jesus spoke about in Matthew 15:7-9. In speaking with the woman at the well in John 4:24, Jesus says, "God is spirit, and those who worship Him must worship in spirit and truth." God wants us to worship in spirit—with our hearts—and in truth—in the ways God has commanded. God looks at the heart of the worshiper, and it is the heart that makes the worship acceptable to Him. Anyone can perform acts of worship, but if the heart is not what is driving the worship, then they worship in vain. The worship is empty.

All God's creation is called to worship, and that includes the angels. In Revelation 5:11-12, we see at least 100 million angels worshiping Christ on the throne. Satan was an angel. He was one of the morning stars of heaven. He seems to have even had a title— "son of the dawn" (Isaiah 14:12, NIV). He was to be a worshiper of God and Christ; however, he was not content to worship. What he really wanted was to sit on the throne and be the object of worship. For this, for not wanting to worship God and for wanting to take God's place as the one to be worshiped, Satan was thrown out of heaven and took up residence on earth. Jesus was there; He saw it. In Luke 10:18, Jesus says, "I saw Satan fall from heaven like lightning" (NIV). Part of worship is bowing down before God in recognition of our place before the Creator. Satan may have been bowing down before God, but his heart was certainly not doing the same.

When Satan was cast down to earth, his desire to be worshiped came with him. That's what the temptation of Adam and Eve was all about. He wanted to cause them to doubt that God can be trusted and that He will do what He says He will do, so they would worship him instead. He tried the same thing with Jesus when Jesus went out into the desert after His baptism, (Matthew 4:1-11). Satan starts out by trying to get Jesus to doubt that God will take care of Him. He is extremely hungry after fasting for 40 days. Satan, knowing this, suggests that Jesus turn the stones into bread. In other words, "God hasn't taken care of you. You must take care of yourself. If you're the Son of God, turn these stones to bread." Jesus doesn't give in. He relies on the Word of God instead. Then Satan tries to get Jesus to test God — to see if He will do what He says He will do in His Word. Again, Jesus puts His trust in God. The final temptation gets at what Satan is really after. He offers Jesus all the kingdoms of the world if he will only bow down and worship him. Jesus says He will worship no one but God, and Satan leaves. We need to take worship as seriously as God does. The first two commandments of the Ten Commandments are about worshiping God and Him alone. He threw Satan out of heaven over worship. The only one worthy of worship is God Himself. He spoke everything into existence and deserves our worship. This was not news to Satan, yet he still wanted to take the place of God and paid the price for it.

Satan has not changed. He is still after worship. He will do anything to get us to worship him instead of God. You're probably thinking, *There is no way I will ever worship Satan!* Unfortunately, the truth is, we all have and will worship Satan. Let me explain. We cannot see it, but there is a spiritual war going on around us. This war is between the forces of Satan — the demons, and the forces of God — the angels. The war is being fought over humanity. God desires to save all of humanity, and Satan desires to condemn all of humanity with himself in hell. Jesus made it quite clear in Matthew 12:30 that there are only two choices in this life concerning worship. Jesus said, "He who is not with Me is against Me; and he who does not gather with Me scatters." We are either with Jesus or against Jesus. There is no middle ground. If we are not with Jesus, then who are we with? There is only one answer — the Enemy, Satan. Jesus said in Luke 16:13 that "No servant can serve two masters; for either he will hate the one and love the other, or else he will be devoted to one and despise the other. You cannot serve God and wealth." Though He was talking about money in this case, the principle is the same for anything we put before God. We cannot divide our worship or devotion between Jesus and anything else. When we give our devotion to something other than God, we are then serving Satan (Matthew 4:10; Deuteronomy 6:13-15). God demands and deserves all our devotion, our wholehearted worship.

Whenever we are doing something outside of God's will, we are serving Satan. There are two choices in this life — worship God or worship Satan. This is the same choice Eve had in the garden and it is the same choice each person faces today. God makes the choice clear for us in Deuteronomy 30:19-20a. "This day I call the heavens and the earth as witnesses against you that I have set before you life and death, blessings and curses. Now choose life, so that you and your children may live and that you may love the LORD your God, listen to his voice, and hold fast to him. For the LORD is your life" (NIV). **Though these words were spoken to Israel, they have meaning for us as well. As Christians, we chose life. We decided to worship God and Him alone. This is a choice each one of us must make anew every day. This is worship, to offer ourselves up to God completely, as said in Romans 12:1-2. Every day, we are to recognize our place before God, to stand in awe of His power, love, mercy, and grace, and give Him all the glory, honor, and praise He deserves.**

The term *quiet time* is familiar to us. It is something Christians are encouraged to have daily. I think it would be better to call it *worship time*. People often say that our entire lives are worship. We should do everything to the glory of God, and I agree. However, I think God wants focused worship from each of us as well, and not just on Sunday morning. We should worship God every day, giving Him the praise and honor He deserves. We should be open with Him in prayer, sacrificing time to just "be still" with Him, listening for His whisper, reading His Word with eagerness, and singing songs of praise. With each new day, we should open our hearts to Him, placing them once again on the altar as a sacrifice and aroma pleasing to God, and in turn, placing God once again on the throne in our lives. That is true worship.

One evening, I was giving my grandchildren piano lessons. While my granddaughter, Julia, waited for her turn, she kept herself busy with her crayons, paper, and sequins. Finally, it was her turn for a lesson. When she sat on the piano bench, she proudly gave me a drawing of herself, me, and the piano.

Above the piano she had written, "I can play piano." In the bottom corner of the paper, she had written "turn over!" On the back she had written, "Grandma, you are the best piano teacher ever! I love you." Julia gave me that picture because she wanted me to know how much she loved and appreciated me. The picture was a child's drawing, not that of an accomplished artist. But it was the most beautiful picture to me because it came from her heart. I will cherish that picture forever. I don't think God is much different when it comes to worship from His children. True worship comes from our hearts. It may not be perfect or accomplished, but for God, giving Him our hearts far outshines any other offering we could give. So, let's worship Him in spirit and in truth, with our hearts and actions, because true worship really does take heart.

Bold Points to Ponder

- How did you measure success before becoming a Christian? Looking back, do you see yourself as a rebel in relation to God? What has changed?

- What are some things people worship today? What are some of the things you "worship" in your life, other than Christ?

- Read Romans 1:18-25. What does this scripture warn against? (Pay special attention to verses 23 and 25)

  - Describe some examples of people worshiping created things rather than the Creator.

- ◆ Share some examples of how Christians might fall into this same worship trap. How do we avoid this trap? (Psalm 19:9-10)

- Read Philippians 4:4, Psalm 1:1-3, and Psalm 19:8. Where is true happiness found?

- Read Matthew 6:24-34. What kind of negative impact does worshiping other things or people have on our lives?

- Read Acts 14:8-20. Who were the people worshiping and why?

  - ◆ What are the dangers of putting another Christian on a pedestal? What risks come from allowing yourself to be put on a pedestal by others?

- Read 1 Peter 4:10-11 and Matthew 5:16. How do these verses pertain to worship? (Keep in mind what is said in Revelation 4:9-11)

  - ◆ On a scale of 1 to 10, how would you rate the current state of your worship — both in attitude and action? What changes can you make to bring you closer to a "10"?

  - ◆ What can you do to make sure you're not just going through the motions but are worshiping Him with the same heart and zeal that you did when you first became a Christian?

  - ◆ Read 2 Corinthians 10:4-5. Our own thoughts are one of the biggest distractions for many of us. Is this a challenge for you? What can you do about it? What does the Scripture say to do about it?

- Bowing before the Lord in worship requires humility. Read James 4:7-10 and 1 Peter 5:6. Reflect on your worship, both on Sunday morning and throughout the week.

  - Do you "purify your heart" before you worship? How do you do that?

  - How do you approach worship on Sunday? Daily?

- Have you put other things before worshiping God? Have you had a divided heart? If so, what do you need to do in order to put worshiping God back in first place where it belongs?

12

Offer Your Service

If there was anything unusual on this particular Sunday morning, I wasn't aware of it. I got up, ate some yogurt, showered, and headed out the door to worship service, just like I'd done thousands of times before. Once at the building, I found a seat and settled in for some singing. As is our custom, after the first song and some announcements, we took a few minutes to leave our seats and greet one another. I talked to a few people and, with only a few seconds remaining, gave one last woman a hug and spoke with her. With God, all it takes is a few seconds to change your life, and that's what He did for me. This Sunday didn't start out differently from any others, but it is a Sunday I will never forget because it forever changed my thoughts about worship.

You're probably wondering what happened in those 15-20 seconds to impact me so deeply — I'll share it in just a moment.

When we talked about our individual worship, we discussed how we are to be an offering to God every day. God commands us to live for Him daily. Part of our daily worship is spending time with Him in His Word and in prayer. He desires intimacy with us, and the habit of a daily quiet time helps us to achieve that intimacy. Individual worship of God is commanded, but so is a time when all His believers gather to worship Him together. We call it corporate worship, and our designated time for it is every Sunday morning.

Think about your Sunday morning worship. If it's anything like mine, you sing, pray, have the Lord's Supper, a sermon, a collection for the needs of the congregation, and fellowship. In doing some research, I found this to be much like the worship services in the first and second centuries. God gives us a description in Acts 2:42. It says, "They were continually devoting themselves to the apostles' teaching and to fellowship, to the breaking of bread and to prayer." I also found a description of a typical worship service written by Justin Martyr, who lived in the early second century:

> "On the day called Sunday, there is a gathering together in the same place of all who live in a given city or rural district. The memoirs of the apostles or the writings of the prophets are read, as long as time permits. Then when the reader ceases, the president in a discourse admonishes and urges the imitation of these good things. Next, we all rise together and send up prayers. When we cease from our prayer, bread is presented and wine and water. The president in the same manner sends up prayers and thanksgivings, according to his ability, and the people sing out their assent, saying the 'Amen.' A distribution and participation of the elements for which thanks have been given is made to each person, and to those who are not present they are sent by the deacons. Those who have means and are willing, each

according to his own choice, gives what he wills, and what is collected is deposited with the president. He provides for the orphans and widows, those who are in need on account of sickness or some other cause, those who are in bonds, strangers who are sojourning, and in a word, he becomes the protector of all who are in need."

(Christianity Today)

In the above description, we can see most of the elements of our worship service today — the reading of Scripture, a sermon, the Lord's Supper, prayer, and a collection. As the goal of the churches of Christ is to be like the first-century church as much as possible, it is encouraging to see how similar our services are to those in the mid-second century. We are doing the right things, but something concerns me. How often do we do all the right things in worship service, but don't truly worship? Is worship service another area in our lives we've done so many times that we now go through the service on auto-pilot?

I know there have been times I've sung all the songs, listened to the sermon, took the Lord's Supper, put money in the collection plate, and prayed, but didn't worship. I was on auto-pilot — doing all the right things but without engaging my heart. Jesus said in Mark 7:6, "Rightly did Isaiah prophesy of you hypocrites, as it is written: 'THIS PEOPLE HONORS ME WITH THEIR LIPS, BUT THEIR HEART IS FAR AWAY FROM ME.'" Just as our minds often wander in our personal time with God, our minds wander in corporate worship. We may sit in the pew, performing all the right tasks while thinking of what we will have for dinner, chores needing to be done, one more item to add to our grocery list, or even worse, using our phones to check email, social media, or text someone. We sing the songs without even thinking about the words we are singing and take part in the Lord's Supper as if it is an item on a checklist. God wants, and deserves, more than that from us. He wants us to worship Him in spirit and truth. He wants more than the correct actions in worship. He wants the involvement of our hearts.

My firm belief is that none of us do any of this on purpose. We don't plan on being only a spectator in the worship service. However, it happens all too frequently. How can we prevent ending up on auto-pilot? Look with me at Exodus 19:9, "The Lord said to Moses, 'Behold, I will come to you in a thick cloud, so that the people may hear when I speak with you and may also believe in you forever.' Then Moses told the words of the people to the Lord." **And in verses 14-17,** "So Moses went down from the mountain to the people and consecrated the people, and they washed their garments. He said to the people, 'Be ready for the third day; do not go near a woman.' So it came about on the third day, when it was morning, that there were thunder and lightning flashes and a thick cloud upon the mountain and a very loud trumpet sound, so that all the people who were in the camp trembled. And Moses brought the people out of the camp to meet God, and they stood at the foot of the mountain."

Get Ready

We have a few things to learn from this passage, the most important is that the Jews took three days to prepare to meet God. Here's a question I've asked myself and really didn't like my answer. How much time do you take to prepare to meet God on Sunday morning? Do you prepare at all? I've already shared with you my Sunday morning routine — food, shower, dress, drive to the building, find my seat, and settle in. Those things are nothing special. I do the same things when I go to work. Somehow, I think going to worship God should differ from getting ready for work.

Another question I would like you to answer honestly with yourself is, *When you're getting ready for worship service, do you take time to think about the fact that you are getting ready to meet with God?* Take a minute to take that question in and truly consider it. Every Sunday morning, we have the privilege of meeting with the Creator of the Universe, the Creator who made us, the Creator who sacrificed His Son for us. Just thinking about this as I wrote the last sentence filled me with such awe. Who am I that God would want to meet with me?

In the Scripture I referenced above from Exodus 19, in addition to seeing their preparation, we see the reaction of the Israelites when God met them on the mountain. Scripture says "all the people who were in the camp trembled." Then they followed Moses out to the foot of the mountain to meet God. They understood the magnitude of what was happening. We need that same understanding as we go out to our buildings to meet God. There is nothing routine about it, but we act like it's just another day. Like the Israelites, we should prepare ourselves to meet with God and understand the magnitude of what we are doing. I'll share with you some ideas I have on how to prepare for worship, some practical and some spiritual.

The first idea is practical: Prepare the night before. I know a woman who had eight young children she was raising on her own. Knowing she had to get everyone ready and out the door in time for worship on Sunday, she spent time every Saturday night preparing. She bathed the children and laid out the clothes for each of them, making sure they were all clean and pressed. She got out the dishes and silverware necessary for breakfast and planned what everyone would eat. Because she prepared on Saturday, on Sunday her family ate, cleaned up, dressed, and was ready for worship on time. God said for the Israelites to wash their clothes and be prepared, and that is just what she did and what we can do, too.

Besides being physically prepared, it is important to be spiritually prepared. I no longer roll out of bed, get ready, and leave.

Now, I get up a little early so that I can start my morning with the Lord. I take some time to say good morning to God in prayer and then listen for His voice in the Scriptures. Doing this has made my church worship time even more meaningful. It puts me in the right frame of mind to meet with the Lord along with my church family. Just because it's Sunday and we attend worship service does not mean we can ignore our personal worship time with Him. God wants to hear our praise and worship as a congregation, but He also wants to commune with us individually. Find what works for you to prepare yourself spiritually to meet with God. You'll be amazed at the positive effect it will have on your corporate worship.

Another idea for preparing spiritually comes from Matthew 5:23-24, where Jesus says, "Therefore if you are presenting your offering at the altar, and there remember that your brother has something against you, leave your offering there before the altar and go; first be reconciled to your brother, and then come and present your offering." When we go to worship God on Sunday morning, we are worshiping Him individually and as a group. If we have a fractured relationship with one of our fellow Christians, it affects not only us but the entire body. Jesus wants us to heal our relationships, make amends, before we offer Him our praise, prayers, and offerings. His desire is for us to be one and to worship Him with love for Him and one another. Take an honest assessment of your relationships before going to worship. If you've been wronged, forgive; if you've wronged someone else, ask God's forgiveness and resolve to seek the forgiveness of the one you've wronged. Remember that Jesus said they will know we are His because of our love for each other. There are so many verses commanding us to love one another. Do not let another day go by without reaching out to heal broken relationships, so the body can truly worship as one.

Our church relationships are not the only relationships we need to assess. Before taking the Lord's Supper, we should examine ourselves and ask forgiveness for any sin hindering our relationship with God. Paul writes in 1 Corinthians 11:26-29, "For as often as you eat this bread and drink the cup, you proclaim the Lord's death until He comes. Therefore whoever eats the bread or drinks the cup of the Lord in an unworthy manner, shall be guilty of the body and the blood of the Lord. But a man must examine himself, and in so doing he is to eat of the bread and drink of the cup. For he who eats and drinks, eats and drinks judgment to himself if he does not judge the body rightly." It is a privilege to take part in the Lord's Supper, but it is another section of the worship service that can become routine. We must not let it. Use the time for self-examination, and instead of the Lord's Supper being routine, it becomes intensely personal. Think of the unspeakable horror of Jesus' death on the cross, and this part of the worship service is not only personal, it is intimate. It's just you and God. Identify any sin in your life. Before eating the bread and drinking the cup, approach God in prayer with a truly repentant heart and seek His forgiveness. Then when you take the Lord's Supper, it will be with a pure heart and a clean conscience. If we all approach the Lord's Supper in this manner, it would strengthen us and the church body.

Define Your "Why"

If I asked you why you go to worship service each week, you might say something like this: to fulfill a command, because it's expected of you, to have the Lord's Supper, or because you like the preacher and his sermons. Why do we worship together? Well, we saw in Acts 4 that the first-century church met together to hear the apostles' teaching, have the Lord's Supper, to fellowship, and to pray. Since we are modeling ourselves after the church in the Bible, we do the same. Yes, that is part of it, but see what Scripture says in Hebrews 10:24, 25. "and let us consider how to stimulate one another to love and good deeds, not forsaking our own assembling together, as is the habit of some, but encouraging one another; and all the more as you see the day drawing near." Scripture says not to give up meeting together (NIV), and in the NASB it says "not forsaking our own assembling together." It is important to God that we meet together — in fact, it is a command.

I know of people who say they can meet with God anywhere and they don't need to go to church. Well, Scripture disagrees with them for some good reasons. We do not go to worship service only to worship God and take part in the Lord's Supper. Those are two important reasons we go, but the Scripture in Hebrews is about more than that. Perhaps one of the most important reasons we worship together is to "stimulate one another" to live the life Jesus has called us to live.

It is true, we can meet with God anywhere, but He wants us to meet with Him alongside His people. God knows we need one another. Scripture says we are to encourage one another when we assemble together. That is why He wants us to worship Him together, as one body, as people who love the Lord. He wants us to extend His love to others and encourage each other not to give up, but to keep our eyes on Jesus and our place in heaven. This is part of fellowship and an extremely important part of Sunday worship.

Okay, so it's time I tell you what happened that Sunday morning. when God, in just a few seconds, profoundly changed my view of Sunday worship. As I told you, I was greeting people, and with only a few seconds left, I hugged a woman and asked her this question: "Is there anything I can pray about for you?" The pain and desperation I heard in her voice as she answered broke my heart. She told me that two of her family members had been killed during the week, and she needed prayer, as did her family. She didn't understand why they were taken in such a way. Fighting back tears, I assured her I would pray and hugged her again, telling her to call me if she needed anything at all. She answered, "Just prayer. Please pray."

In those few seconds, God opened my eyes to why I need to be at Sunday worship service every week. Yes, I can worship God anywhere, but in that building on Sunday morning, there are people in need of love, prayer, encouragement, and even hugs. At times, I have been the one in need of those things, and I am so grateful to God that He provides a time each week for those needs to be met. The world might beat us down a bit during the week, but we have Sunday to anticipate. On Sunday, we are reminded that we are not alone. Not only do we have Jesus, but we have each other.

Take the time to talk with each other. I don't mean complimenting someone on their outfit, their new hairstyle, or sharing about the latest movie you saw. Instead, why not share about what you've been reading in the Bible and what God has been showing you? Listen as they share what they've been learning and discuss Scripture with them. It is encouraging to hear what God is teaching others, and what you share with others will encourage them. And I have learned that perhaps the most important question you can ask someone is, "What can I pray about for you?" It's then, when they realize someone really cares, that people will pour out their hearts — their deepest fears, worries, concerns, and needs. Pray for and with them, fulfilling the commands to love one another, pray for one another, and encourage one another. Obeying those commands has the power to change each one of us in profound ways, bringing us closer to each other and to God.

Worshiping God on Sunday is not a spectator sport. If you've been a spectator, it is time to get in the game. God wants us engaged in worship, having our hearts open to Him as we sing, pray, take the Lord's Supper, listen to the sermon, and fellowship with one another. Preparing on Saturday for Sunday morning worship, starting the day alone with God before service, examining our spiritual condition and relationships before meeting with God, and examining ourselves before taking the Lord's Supper, takes us off autopilot and enables us to worship the way God commands—in spirit and in truth. And when the worship service is over, don't run right out of the building. If you do, you will miss one of the best parts of worshiping together, giving and receiving encouragement from each other. God knows we all need it, and hopefully, now you know, too.

....

Bold Points to Ponder

- What, if any, is the connection between your personal worship and your corporate worship? How does one affect the other?

- Read Exodus 19:9-17. List some of your observations about meeting with God from the text and discuss how you can apply your observations to your own Sunday morning meetings with God.

- Read Psalm 8:1-4; Psalm 144:3-4; 1 Peter 2:9-11. What do these Scriptures tell you about who you are to God?

- Read Psalm 27:8; James 4:7-9; Jeremiah 33:2-3; Matthew 7:7-8; Matthew 11:27-28.

- What do these verses teach about approaching God? Discuss how you might feel has hindered you from approaching Him?

- Read Hebrews 12:28, Psalm 96:7-9, and Psalm 100. Explain what these verses tell you about the importance of worship. How should you approach worship?

- Preparing physically for worship on Sunday is not difficult, but how do you prepare spiritually to meet God?

- Have you ever gone through times when the Lord's Supper was "routine?" If so, how did you get out of the "routine" and become engaged again?

  - What do you think about during the Lord's Supper?

- Share a time you experienced real encouragement and renewed confidence to live as God commands because of attending worship and conversing with another Christian there.

- This Sunday, ask someone "What can I pray about for you?" and write down what you discover by asking that simple question.

13

Nearer to God

My husband and I walked into the worship service, hand in hand, a little later than usual that Sunday morning. We slipped into our seats, still clasping hands, and tried to keep our minds on the service. With each song, I fought back tears and wrestled my mind back to where I knew it should be — on worshiping God. The feel of my husband's hand giving mine a gentle squeeze brought fresh tears to my eyes and a prayer to my heart. I honestly couldn't tell you what was said in the sermon, or anything else about the service that day, but one thing I can tell you is that I began a new journey that morning—a journey of renewal in my understanding of the blessing and privilege it is to go to God in prayer.

Without noticing it, my prayer life and my prayers had changed. Like other areas of my Christian life, my passion for prayer had slowly waned and become stale. If you and I were sitting face to face talking about our prayer lives, I wouldn't be surprised if our experiences were similar. The night I gave my life to Christ in baptism was one I'll never forget. After my baptism, we all went to a friend's home and had a celebration. What is better to celebrate than a new sister in Christ? Though I enjoyed the party, it wasn't long before I slipped outside and took a short walk. I needed to be alone with God. The sky was clear, and the stars were amazingly bright. As I walked, I talked with God, pouring out my heart and giving Him thanks and praise for adopting me into His family. I was in awe that I could speak with Him in this way and that He was eager to listen to what I had to say. Somewhere along the way, I had lost that sense of wonder. That Sunday morning, fighting back tears, I began to regain what had slipped away.

If I'm honest, God had used more than one experience to bring me back to praying as I should. One experience I will never forget occurred on April 15, 2013. It was a beautiful spring day with a brilliant blue sky — a day you expect only good things to happen. At 2:49 pm, however, evil showed itself. I was usually at the finish line when my husband ran a race, but this time the train to get there was late. Instead, I was waiting for him in the family meet-up area. Suddenly, there was a loud boom. Looking up at the clear sky, I knew it couldn't have been thunder. I turned to the woman next to me and said, "That sounded like a bomb." She laughed at me and assured me it was only thunder. It was then the second boom rang out, and the ground shook.

Out of the corner of my eye, I saw movement. I turned to look and saw a police officer running as fast as he could with a look of horror on his face. That look is forever etched in my mind. I knew two things at that instant — the Boston Marathon had been bombed, and my husband had just crossed the finish line.

I began walking as fast as I could toward that finish line, praying over and over that he had made it through before the bombs went off. My eyes darted back and forth, trying to see around the people in front of me, praying to see him coming toward me without injury. God answered that prayer and the many other prayers we prayed that day as we tried to find a way out of the city. With cellphone signals blocked, God answered my prayer to let my family know we were okay. He allowed one call into my phone — the call from my daughter-in-law in California, crying with relief when she heard we were uninjured. She would let the others know and would continue to pray for us. Later, God answered our prayer of finding a way out of the city, when a young girl we'd spoken with earlier came back to say her parents were headed that way and wanted to give us a ride. As the day passed, I witnessed God's love in a variety of ways, but none more so than His answers to prayers silently spoken from our hearts to His.

That day played a part in renewal of my prayer life. As we walked through the city, searching for a way out, I saw beauty amid the turmoil surrounding us. There in the middle of a sidewalk were eight or nine people in a circle, hands clasped, praying. I stopped for a moment, listening to their prayers and adding my own to theirs. Seeing faith in the face of evil was striking and encouraging. I was a witness to God's people, praying in faith, and God answering those prayers in ways I would never have predicted. Like the night of my baptism, I felt God's presence and the awe that not only was He listening to my prayers — He was walking along the streets of Boston with me.

What Prayer Can Do

Relationship; that's what prayer is all about. As a new Christian, I knew that instinctively. Back then, my prayers were me talking with God. How I worded my thoughts didn't concern me. I spoke from my heart as I would to a cherished friend. My prayers were personal and real. For me, prayer was sharing my life with God and trusting Him to guide me; that's relationship. Over the years, hearing so many others pray changed how I spoke with God in prayer. Unconsciously, I adopted the words and phrases I'd heard others use. They weren't wrong, but they weren't mine. I needed to get my heart engaged again in prayer, and God used the incidents above to reach me.

Has your prayer life become stale? Do your prayers lack passion? Do you long for that close relationship with God through prayer that you had as a new Christian? You are not alone, but how do we recapture it? The first step is to remind ourselves of the privilege we have in approaching God in prayer and the reason for that privilege. You see, though everyone can pray, not all will have their prayers answered. Isaiah 59:1-2 says, "Behold, the LORD's hand is not so short That it cannot save; Nor is His ear so dull That it cannot hear. But your iniquities have made a separation between you and your God, And your sins have hidden His face from you so that He does not hear." God hears all prayers, because God sees and hears everything, but this verse makes clear that sin separates a person from God and hides God's face from them. In 1 Peter 3:12, we see this even more clearly, "For the eyes of the lord are toward the righteous, and his ears attend to their prayer, but the face of the lord is against those who do evil." In this scripture, we see that God's eyes are on the righteous, those who belong to Him, and He hears their prayers. However, those who do what is evil, who do not belong to Him in Christ, His face turns against or away from them. God hears them, but He doesn't recognize them as His children. Approaching God and having Him hear and answer our prayers is a right given only to His children.

What makes us righteous? What makes us His? We know we can't make ourselves right with God, because we are all sinners deserving of death (Romans 6:23). We need our sins forgiven, and the only way that happens is by believing in Jesus and being washed in His blood. Ephesians 1:7 says, "In Him we have redemption through His blood, the forgiveness of our trespasses, according to the riches of His grace."

Forgiveness of our sins comes through the sacrifice of Jesus, through His blood. That blood cleanses us of sin and makes us righteous in the eyes of God. When we come up out of the waters of baptism, God no longer sees us as sinners; instead, He sees us as righteous and His children. Because we belong to Him through Christ, we can approach Him in prayer, knowing He hears us and will answer us. God sacrificed His Son, who suffered immeasurably when He took on our sins and punishment on the cross. They did all of this so that we can have an intimate relationship with God. God so desires fellowship with us, that He made a way for us to fellowship with Him. Knowing how much God sacrificed and Jesus suffered for us to speak with God should fill us with awe, gratefulness, and humility. What a privilege and blessing it is to be God's child and for us to call Him, Father!

In the Name of Jesus

Prayer is a privilege full of power, but it is too often neglected. Exercising our right to approach God's throne in prayer connects us to His power. It is there we come into contact with His mercy and grace. Because we belong to Christ, we can speak with God in the name of Jesus, under His authority. In Hebrews 4:14 and 16, Scripture says, "Therefore, since we have a great high priest who has passed through the heavens, Jesus the Son of God, let us hold fast our confession…Therefore let us draw near with confidence to the throne of grace, so that we may receive mercy and find grace to help in time of need."

We can approach God with confidence because we have believed in Jesus and belong to Him. Without Jesus, we would have no confidence in approaching God. Whenever we close our prayers with the words, "in Jesus' name," this is more than a ritual; it is full of meaning. Let me give you an example. When a representative of a leader from another country comes to the United States and meets with the President, he does so in the name of the foreign leader. He comes under the authority of the one over him and because of that authority, he is accepted and allowed to meet with the President. It is the same with us, because we come and ask things of God in Jesus' name, under His authority, we are accepted before the throne of God as one of His children. So, you see those three words mean everything in the eyes of God and are the foundation of our relationship with Him.

Another word that describes our relationship with God is *child*. We are His children. John writes in 1 John 3:1, "See how great a love the Father has bestowed on us, that we would be called children of God; and such we are. For this reason the world does not know us, because it did not know Him." You can almost hear John's amazement and feel the excitement he felt as he wrote those words. John was in awe of being God's child, and we should be as well. We have already said that we can approach the throne of God because of this relationship, but being God's child should also affect our prayers in another way. Let's look at Mark 10:13-15. "And they were bringing children to Him so that He might touch them; but the disciples rebuked them. But when Jesus saw this, He was indignant and said to them, 'Permit the children to come to Me; do not hinder them; for the kingdom of God belongs to such as these. Truly I say to you, whoever does not receive the kingdom of God like a child will not enter it at all.'" We often use these verses to show how much Jesus loves children and that we are to care for them and teach them about Jesus and living for Him. That is true, but for our purposes, I would like us to look at them because we are the children — God's children.

When I was a little girl, I believed that my father could do absolutely anything. No matter what I asked of him, he could do it. I had this reassurance because I knew I could depend on my dad for anything. This is the relationship we have with our Father, God. When we pray, we should pray as a little child, sharing what is on our hearts, and expecting God will answer our prayers. Unlike my father, our God can do anything. When I first became a Christian, I prayed with expectation. I prayed with confidence because I knew my God was all-powerful. Speaking with God in prayer, I presented my requests and spoke of the deepest things in my heart. It never occurred to me that God wouldn't listen and answer my prayers. As I write these words, I can feel that confidence, peace, and closeness I experienced in prayer with God back then. Somewhere along the way, my prayers began to lack that same confidence and assurance.

For many, the powerful prayers they once prayed with confidence and expectation have become prayers of routine and doubt. They think, *Who am I? Why should God answer my prayer?* When this happened to me, I realized I had become like the person James speaks of in James 1:5-8, who doubts even as she prays. The doubts had overtaken my prayers, tossed me about, and stolen the power from them. I had lost my childlike faith, the faith that says there is nothing my God cannot and will not do. Here is the good news, it is possible to find that faith again.

Some years ago, a friend of mine was pregnant, and she desperately wanted a girl. She already had two boys, and she was praying daily for God to give her a healthy baby girl. She was adamant that God was going to answer her prayer. I tried talking with her about what she would do, how she would feel, if God said "no" and instead gave her a healthy baby boy. She refused to even consider it. She "knew" God would give her a girl. She prayed without doubt throughout the entire pregnancy. She bought all pink things, did the nursery with a girl in mind, and only picked out a girl's name for the baby. When the day came for her to give birth, God blessed her with the girl for whom she had diligently prayed. It was no surprise to her because she truly believed and trusted that God would answer her prayer. She was God's child and prayed with the innocence and faith of a child to a God who responded as a loving father. She prayed with faith, trust, confidence, and the persistence only a child can muster. God doesn't always answer yes, like He did for my friend, but we should always approach Him with our heartfelt requests with faith that doesn't doubt, with confidence, and with expectation. God will answer, and regardless of how He answers our prayers, we can be confident that He always loves us.

While we bring our requests to God, we also go to Him seeking His forgiveness. Though we belong to Christ, we must fight daily against sin in our lives. James wrote in James 1:13-15, "Let no one say when he is tempted, 'I am being tempted by God'; for God cannot be tempted by evil, and He Himself does not tempt anyone. But each one is tempted when he is carried away and enticed by his own lust. Then when lust has conceived, it gives birth to sin; and when sin is accomplished, it brings forth death." Notice that James did not say "if" tempted; he said "when" tempted. We are all tempted by our own fleshly desires and must fight against giving in and falling into sin. Unfortunately, there will be times when we give into sin. This is no surprise to God, that's why He's given us the privilege of prayer in Jesus' name. He is waiting to forgive us and set us back on the path of righteousness. God sees us as His children and will always be there for us. We read in Mark 10:13-15 about Jesus letting the little children come to Him. Verse 16 says, "And He took them in His arms and began blessing them, laying His hands on them." Reading this verse, picturing myself as the child, a memory from many years ago comes to mind.

When I was a small child, I disobeyed my father, and he punished me for it. I remember being furious with him. In my childish mind, I justified what I'd done and blamed him for being "so mean" to me. I spent the rest of the day in my room, nursing my anger. When it was time for bed, I ignored my routine of saying goodnight to my father and giving him a kiss on the cheek. My mother came to my room and told me I needed to go say goodnight to him. She told me I had hurt his feelings, and he was sad. Grudgingly, I went downstairs to the family room, said goodnight, and turned to go to bed. He stopped me, and I turned, expecting to get a lecture. Instead, he gently lifted me onto his lap and wrapped his arms around me. As I slowly gave up my anger and snuggled into his embrace, he explained that even when I did something wrong and he punished me, he still loved me. He didn't punish me to hurt me; he punished me because he loved me and wanted the best for me. I told him I was sorry, with tears running down my cheeks. "You're forgiven," he said. He hugged me again, kissed my cheek, and with a last "I love you," sent me to bed. I remember feeling joyful and relieved. Forgiveness gives a new, positive outlook to life.

Just as Jesus did when He took the little children in His arms, my dad had wrapped his arms around me and changed everything with his love. We never need to be afraid to confess our sins to God and seek His forgiveness. He loves us and wants the best for us. We can trust that when we confess our sins, He will forgive us. He is eager to forgive and restore our relationship. We have this assurance found in 1 John 1:9, "If we confess our sins, He is faithful and righteous to forgive us our sins and to cleanse us from all unrighteousness." Confessing our sins to God and seeking His forgiveness are privileges and a big part of prayer. Some people avoid prayer when they find themselves steeped in sin or full of guilt. Satan is giddy when we do that. Instead of trying to hide from God, which is impossible anyway, we need to seek Him out. Guilt and shame will have no power over us once we bring it all to God.

Focus on the Father

The last thing I want to mention concerning prayer has to do with what Jesus says in Matthew 6:5-6. "When you pray, you are not to be like the hypocrites; for they love to stand and pray in the synagogues and on the street corners so that they may be seen by men. Truly I say to you, they have their reward in full. But you, when you pray, go into your inner room, close your door and pray to your Father who is in secret, and your Father who sees [what is done] in secret will reward you." Jesus is warning us here not to do our praying for show. He never meant prayer for that. There is no place for pride in prayer. Verse 8 of Matthew 6 tells us, "your Father knows what you need before you ask him." So why do we need to ask Him? Just like when my children were young, and I kept my eye on them from the window, hearing everything that went on, God sees and hears what goes on in our lives, too. Even though I already knew what had transpired, I listened attentively when my children would relay the day's events to me. I already knew, but it gave me joy to have them share their experiences with me. It brought us closer. That is what prayer is all about — relationship. God doesn't need us to tell Him what we need, but He wants us to tell Him because

He wants a relationship with us. When we go into our room, or the place we set aside for prayer, it becomes a place of intimate conversation. Shutting everything else out, we can focus completely on speaking with our Father, all the while being sure He is listening with interest.

Prayer. It's so much more than a collect call to the Creator of the universe. It's more than asking Him to fulfill your wishes like a cosmic bellhop. God has shown me this over and over again. I guess I'm a slow learner. In the beginning of this chapter, I shared with you a difficult Sunday morning service that helped to get me on this journey of renewal and growth of my prayer life. That Sunday was just a few days after my husband and I learned he had a brain tumor requiring surgery, or it would eventually end his life. We had told no one yet and wouldn't until we had told our children. Instead, we leaned on each other and on the One who we knew was there for us. Yes, we prayed for healing, protection, and wisdom. We presented our requests to God. But more than that, we poured our hearts out to Him. We spoke with Him on an intimate level, sharing our pain, fear, and faith. Knowing He was in control gave us such comfort. God watched over my husband and answered many prayers in the ensuing months, but that's a story for another time. Suffice it to say, His hand was clearly on every step of that journey.

My prayer journey continues today, and I am striving to have the personal relationship with God in prayer that He intends. I am trying to be the child who shares her life with her Father and listens for His voice daily. The reminder that we are His children that He loves to put His arms around and care for is one we need to keep in the forefront of our minds. We have the privilege of going to God with confidence, faith, and trust in the fact He hears and answers our prayers because we belong to Jesus. We are God's children. He wants to love us, forgive us, and bless us through prayer. Let's make it a habit of going into our "private room" and spending time with the Father in prayer. He's waiting.

Bold Points to Ponder

- What are your feelings and thoughts about prayer? Why do you pray? What do you believe is the purpose of prayer?

- Read Acts 4:29-31. The ground might not have shaken, but describe a time when you knew without a shadow of a doubt that God heard you and was answering your prayers.

- Do you agree that prayer is primarily about building and nurturing a relationship with God? Why or why not?

- How have your prayers changed over the years? Have the prayers of others unconsciously influenced how you speak with God in prayer? In what way?

- Read Ephesians 2:13-15 and Hebrews 4:14-16. What do these verses say about our relationship with God and our prayers?

- What makes you righteous in the sight of God? See John 1:12-13, 1 John 2:29-3:1, and 1 John 3:7.

- Read Luke 18:15-17, John 1:12-13, and 1 John 3:1-2. What difference, if any, would thinking of yourself as a little child approaching God, make in your prayer life?

- Reflect on a time when you prayed, bringing your request before God, but in your heart, you doubted He would answer your prayer. Why did you doubt?

- Take a moment to remember a timewhen you went to the Lord with your heart laid bare, seeking His forgiveness. Was it difficult for you to confess? How did you feel after confessing your sin to Him?

  - What can we learn from our experiences of confessing our sins to God?

  - Read Psalm 32:3-5, Colossians 2:13-14, Ephesians 1:5-7, and 1 John 1:9. What do these verses say about confession and forgiveness?

www.ingramcontent.com/pod-product-compliance
Lightning Source LLC
Chambersburg PA
CBHW070121100426
42744CB00010B/1886